Antigone

Sophocles

Antigone

Translated,
with Introduction and Notes, by

Paul Woodruff

Hackett Publishing Company, Inc.
Indianapolis/Cambridge

06 05 04 03 02   2 3 4 5 6 7 8

For further information, please address
   Hackett Publishing Company, Inc.
   P.O. Box 44937
   Indianapolis, IN 46244-0937

   www.hackettpublishing.com

Cover design by Brian Rak and Abigail Coyle.
Interior design by Meera Dash.

Library of Congress Cataloging-in-Publication Data

Sophocles.
     Antigone / Sophocles ; translated, with introduction and
notes, by Paul Woodruff.
         p.   cm.
     Includes bibliographical references.
     ISBN 0-87220-572-X (cloth) — ISBN 0-87220-571-1 (paper)
     1. Antigone (Greek mythology)—Drama.   I. Woodruff,
Paul, 1943–   II. Title.

PA4414.A7 W66 2001
882'.01—dc21   2001039200

Contents

Introduction to *Antigone*

I have been in love with Antigone since I first encountered the play that bears her name. The ideas to which she gives voice are interesting and important, but the young woman is captivating—the character Sophocles created for this play, Antigone, daughter of Oedipus, Antigone who gives up everything to put right something she believes is wrong. I confess this at the outset because it explains why I may not succeed in writing objectively about the play. In what follows, however, I will attempt to show why some scholars think that her original audience must have condemned her as a bad woman, and I will do my best to bring out the good qualities in her antagonist, Creon. But in the end, like Creon's son who plans to marry her, I want to spit in the old man's face. Creon was sensible, fair-minded, and public-spirited, as are many patriarchal figures. But he does not know how to listen to anyone he considers inferior. Teachers who are advisers to young adults know from sad experience that a parent like Creon can drive sons and daughters to acts of violence against themselves. The kindness that does not listen can be lethal.

To my surprise, however, students often prefer Creon to Antigone, and I have to admit that they have a point. Antigone is no better at listening than her uncle, but he has an excuse she does not have. Creon is facing the greatest danger that could befall a city in ancient Greece—civil war. Nothing does more harm in any society than civil conflict, which affects every part of life, destroying not just governments, but families and the moral character of individuals. This particular civil war is especially disturbing because it exposes Creon's city to destruction by external enemies. No wonder Creon concludes that his city is like a ship in stormy weather: if no one puts a strong hand to the steering oar, the ship will capsize or sink. Creon is right about many things. And, by the end of the play, he does reveal some capacity for listening.

The original audience probably did not sympathize strongly with either Antigone or Creon. The play is open-ended enough that people probably responded in various ways. What we know of the history of ideas suggests that typical Athenians would have found things to like in both characters, but that both would have troubled Athenian viewers too much for them to take sides. While this audience probably wavered, as do the chorus during the play, they ultimately would have known that the gods were against Creon, but they had no reason to infer that the gods therefore supported Antigone. We moderns tend to rush to judgment because we don't know what the ancients understood around 442–1 B.C.E. when the play was probably first produced. But Sophocles' audience had heard the background of his story already, and they knew the danger of civil war. So let's begin by reviewing the state of affairs in Thebes before the sun rises on the opening scene of the play when the citizens of Thebes will rejoice, and the battlefield, littered with bodies of dead warriors from both sides, will not have begun to smell.

What Happened before Sunrise

Yesterday, to the horror of the people, a traitor brought an outside enemy down upon the whole city of Thebes. The threat of destruction by fire and sword was very real. Had battle gone against the people of Thebes, the victors might have led women and children into slavery from their burning homes, passing the corpses of their massacred husbands, fathers, sons, and brothers. But Thebes has been saved. Its citizens now breathe freely, though they have not forgotten the terror.

Who brought this terror against Thebes? It was Polyneices, one of two sons of Oedipus, the king who had married his own mother after killing his father, not knowing they were his parents. When Oedipus was disgraced, Polyneices and his brother, Eteoclês, were too young to rule, so their uncle Creon served as regent. After they reached mature years, the brothers were willing to let Creon rule at first, in order to shield the city from the curse that followed their family. But then they fell to quarrelling over which of them would hold a tyrant's power in Thebes. As the elder, Polyneices laid claim, but he was violently ousted by his younger brother Eteoclês. In exile, Polyneices sought refuge in the powerful city of Argos, where he enjoyed the support of the king and married the king's daughter. After mustering a might army, in a fury against Eteoclês and thirsty for the blood of his own people, Polyneices led an army from Argos against his homeland. (This version of the story comes from *Oedipus at Colonus*, 365–81 and 1291–1307.) Thebes was victorious, but the cost was high for the royal family. Before the battle, Creon's elder son, Megareus, was sacrified to ensure success for Thebes. And in the battle, Antigone's two brothers died, each one with the sin of fratricide on his head. They had killed each other.

As the play opens, power has been returned to the young men's uncle, the former regent Creon, a man so suited to the throne that his very name means "ruler." Now that he has taken charge, Thebes should be safe. Besides, a wedding is in the air, though we will not hear of it until well into the play. Creon's only surviving son, Haemon, is engaged to marry Antigone, one of Oedipus' two daughters. Antigone and her sister, Ismene, are now the only surviving children of Oedipus' family. This marriage will tie up loose ends by keeping two of the three surviving young royals in the ruling family. All should be serene.

The Athenian audience, however, would have expected trouble in Thebes. They were steeped in epic tales of this city's tormented myth-history. Antigone represents the last generation of a family that, according to myth, carries a fatal curse. Thebes will not rest easy while any member of this family remains alive within its boundaries. The tale of Antigone's private action against Creon was not well known, but every Athenian knew a different story about unburied dead. In this version, Creon leaves the whole Argive army unburied; then Theseus brings an army from Athens to defeat Thebes and bury the Argive dead. Athenians took great pride in the victory of Theseus, so they would have found this play surprising: no Theseus, no glorious role for the army of Athens. (On the old version, see Griffith 1999, pp. 4–12 and Else 1976.) Besides, Thebes represents many things that Athens is not (see Zeitlin 1990). Athens is a democracy; Thebes favors authoritarian forms of government—monarchy in myth, oligarchy more recently. Athens stood against the imperious Persian invaders fifty years before this play was produced; Thebes shamefully supported the Persian invasion. Athens welcomed Dionysus and his worship at the first opportunity, but (according to myth) Thebes initially rejected him. And Dionysus is held to be the god of joy who presides over the festival of plays in which *Antigone* is staged.

Conflict

In the opening scene, we learn that Creon has decided to reward the brother who defended Thebes but to impose a penalty on the other brother. While Eteoclês will receive a noble funeral, Polyneices will have the punishment that is common for traitors—no burial at all, on pain of death for anyone who attempts to inter the body. Creon had every reason to suppose that he was on safe ground in making this decree. He was making a fair distinction between the two brothers, one that is more or less in keeping with accepted practice.

To be denied the full ritual of burial is shameful, a grievous penalty for a traitor and his family. Normally, however, the body of a slain traitor would not be left as carrion for wild dogs and vultures. Sometimes relatives were allowed to give it a burial outside the city, or sometimes the body was thrown into a pit or into the sea. Either of these methods, while leaving the sting of shame as a penalty, would save the land from the pollution of rotting flesh. Although well known in Athens and elsewhere, the non-burial of traitors raised a number of problems. The unburied dead would be shamed and unable to rest in their assigned places. Their family would carry shame as well, for having left one of the most important family obligations unfulfilled. The land on which the corpse was left would also be affected not just by the unpleasantness of rotting flesh but, more importantly, by what the Greeks called *miasma*—the pollution, a kind of implied curse that spreads over a land that has not treated its dead with propriety. Besides, the gods of the Underworld, principally Hades, are entitled to have the dead in their domain. To keep the dead above ground and to send the living below ground—both of these are affronts to the gods below.

That is why Antigone has decided to shoulder the responsibility of burying her brother Polyneices. In this she goes beyond what is normally expected of women. But there is no man left in the family, aside from Creon, whom Antigone now sees as an enemy. In such a case, a woman could be expected to take on a masculine role. And so the drama unfolds, as a determined young woman falls foul of an unmovable king. This troubled city, Thebes, is not yet free of conflict; violent death is not yet finished with this doomed family. In fact, the king will lose his son, his wife, his niece, and his throne, all in one terrible day.

Antigone stirs the modern imagination like no other play that has come down to us from the ancient world (Steiner 1984). Even today, discussions of the play rapidly become arguments between women and men, between young people and older ones, between religious folk and defenders of secular reason. All of these conflicts and more come to a head in the collision of young, powerless, passionate Antigone against her uncle, the mature, powerful, initially cold-hearted Creon.

Religion, ethics, and even politics are at stake. Antigone sides with divine law against the king's decree. Her gods—such as Hades—are beneath the earth. Creon, on the other hand, speaks for order and respect at the human level. But he is not godless. His god is in the sky—thunder-wielding Zeus—and Creon has only contempt for those who worship the lord of the Underworld, Hades.

Ethically, uncle and niece promote different virtues. Creon tries to enforce a rational sort of justice that takes no notice of family ties and seeks to preserve the health of the city-state (*polis*) above all. So Polyneices, born as Creon's nephew, becomes his uncle's enemy, through subsequent actions that trump original ties of kinship—according to Creon. Antigone, by contrast, is committed totally to reverence, and nothing matters more to her than the particular obligation that she has with a person naturally, by birth. These ties mean far more to her than justice between her brothers; more than the city-state; more, even, than family ties such as marriage, which are chosen under human law and not given to her at birth.

Politics do not interest Antigone, but her resistance to Creon must have been welcome in democratic Athens. Creon is king, sole ruler of Thebes, and he has the character of a tyrant. Antigone stands for values she shares with many of the common people: family, ceremony and, especially, the duty of a family to bury its dead.

The politics of burial at the time *Antigone* was written were turbulent with crosscurrents. The democratic leadership of Athens was trying to reduce the role of women in public mourning and curb the excesses of the rich in funeral displays; this was part of a broader strategy that tried to put loyalty to the city ahead of the family and the extended family ties that were represented in burial rituals. On the other hand, funeral ceremony was of the utmost importance to ordinary Athenians, who took great pride in their claim to have forced Thebes to bury the Argive dead.

We cannot know how active such political concerns were in the minds of Sophocles' audience. In any case, those concerns belonged to Athens, not Thebes, and at the time of performance rather than in the mythic past. But the Theban myth story is political enough, at least as Sophocles shapes it: Antigone's refusal to obey Creon, though not part of a democratic uprising, will bring on the final catastrophe for the royal family, proving to the survivors that leadership must be tempered by advice from those who are led.

Interpretation

Truly, there is a conflict in this play to suit every interest, and *Antigone* has fascinated intellectuals as a drama of ideas. Philosophers love this play and sometimes treat it as if it were a treatise on philosophical ethics in disguise. While historians are fascinated by the light it sheds on the history of ideas, anthropologists are intrigued by its treatment of gender and family issues. Literary critics remind us that *Antigone* is poetry of spectacular beauty, as well as a drama constructed with extraordinary care. There is room for all of these approaches and more in reading this play, but keep in mind that none of them has led to general agreement. The play is still open. The scholars have left each reader and each member of the audience a wide scope for interpretation. This Introduction will give you the basic tools you need to arrive at your own view; if you want to know more, consult the Suggestions for Further Reading section (page xxviii) or the Selected Bibliography (page 66).

The early nineteenth-century German philosopher G.W.F. Hegel prized the play as "that supreme and absolute example of tragedy." He held that Antigone and Creon both serve moral powers that are valid in themselves—family love and the law of the state, respectively. But both characters, Hegel thinks, fail to recognize that these powers are two parts of the whole "moral substance" (Paolucci 1962, p. 325). So Creon and Antigone go wrong in being one-sided, and they may go wrong in particular actions they take as well. When Hegel writes of a synthesis of opposing powers, he does not mean to imply a relaxation of tension. The conflict that Antigone faces will destroy her and the ethical world of which she is a part, because both sides belong to what is right. True, Antigone's conflict will be superseded by a modern one, but the conflict between family and state lives on in ethical consciousness, never to be resolved in itself, and it continues to move the Spirit (see the Appendix, page 63).

Nussbaum argues against harmonious synthesis; on her view, the conflict between Creon and Antigone cannot be resolved, and this is not a bad thing:

> We are asked to see that a conflict-free life would be lacking in value and beauty next to a life in which it is possible for conflict to arise; that part of the value of each claim derives from a special separateness and distinctness that would be eclipsed by

harmonization. That, as Heraclitus put it, justice really is strife: that is, that the tensions that permit this sort of strife to arise are also, at the same time, partly constitutive of the values themselves. (1986, p. 81)

Another family of interpretations depends on the history of ideas. Scholars in this group think that an Athenian audience would have solved the conflict with ease. From what we know of common Athenian moral values in the period, some argue that the audience would have felt from the first scene that Antigone was a bad woman; others contend that the audience would have taken her side even before the play began (see below, page xvii). Some historical scholars take more balanced views. Perhaps, for example, the audience would have rejected both antagonists—Creon as an autocrat and Antigone as an incestuous product of an accursed and incestuous royal family. Both may be seen to be responsible for the catastrophe (Griffith 1999, p. 29). So the historical approach has not led to any greater consensus than has the philosophical.

Readers with more literary interests focus on imagery and characterization. The imagery of the play is dazzling and confusing, especially in the choral odes; still, it forms a pattern that is useful in understanding the play (Goheen 1951). Characterization is a very thorny issue. Virtually every scene shows us a character doing something that runs against our initial expectations; this tendency is so strong that some critics have thought that Sophocles paid no attention to consistency of character. For example, Haemon establishes himself at the start as a dutiful and respectful son:

I am yours, Father. You set me straight,
Give me good advice, and I will follow it.
No marriage will weigh more with me,
Than your good opinion. (635–8)

But before his exit, he is arguing furiously with his father:

Talk, talk, talk! Why don't you ever want to listen? (757)

Was he lying when he said he respected his father? Has he changed during the scene? Was he forced by his father's suspicions to take on new attitudes? Or is he an inconsistent character? On this point, too, there is no firm consensus.

My view (influenced by Reinhardt 1947) is that the characters
are forced to change under the pressure of events, with the result
that the play is highly dynamic. The characters are moving tar-
gets, morally speaking; therefore, in the final analysis, we cannot simply take sides on moral grounds. We love Haemon or we
hate him; but, from this viewpoint, we can't justify our prefer-
ence any more than could an Athenian audience. The ancients
believed, with the chorus, that a person's judgment can be shaken
by the madness Zeus sends, and that to be so shaken is more sad
than blameworthy:

> . . . once a house is shaken by the gods,
> Then madness stalks the family without fail,
> Disaster for many generations.
> It is like a great salt wave
> Kicked up by foul winds from Thrace, . . . (583–7)

If Zeus shakes these characters off course, however, he does so
indirectly. Onstage, we see that they are changed by each other
and by the terrible pressures under which they must decide what
to do. And as one person changes, another must change in
response. Creon grows more and more suspicious once he hears
of the illicit burial, under the fear of resurgent civil war, and
Haemon must react to those rising suspicions with increased independence. When Creon calls his son "a woman's toy, a slave"—
and does so in public (756)—he is delivering a deadly insult. No
wonder that calm, rational Haemon flies into a rage.

Call this the "moving target" theory: Whatever else it conveys,
the play warns against moral complacency. In *Antigone*, people
are tested beyond their limits with catastrophic results. For such
a catastrophe, who is to blame? According to the chorus, Zeus is
in control:

> O Zeus! Who could ever curtail thy power? (604)

So ask the chorus, knowing that no one, not even a lesser god, can
stand against Zeus. Onstage, however, it is not Zeus but Creon
who drives his son crazy. No surprise in that; fathers often drive
their sons crazy. The scene makes sense for any audience, whether
or not they agree with the chorus that Zeus is pulling strings
from behind the scenes. Either way, the outcome is intensely sad.

Sophocles' Artistry: The Form
of Ancient Greek Tragedy

Setting aside problems of interpretation, all parties agree that Sophocles is a master dramatist. *Antigone* is a brilliant stage piece built around human conflicts that carry three people to their deaths and threaten two others. It is a play of characters, all of whom matter as *people* to their audience. Sophocles draws characters so powerfully that we care about them from their first entrances, are touched by them, and come to like them—yes, even Creon.

Besides, the language of the play is ravishing, never dropping to the bare painstaking diction of a debate about ideas. The chorus of elders burst upon us from the start with a breathtaking ode to victory. The poetry Sophocles has given them to sing throughout the play is beautiful beyond a translator's art; yet its images are so concrete and so striking that no translator who carried them honestly across the divide from Greek to a modern language could fail to convey their imaginative power.

What marks the play as poetry is not rhyme (ancient poetry almost never used end rhyme) but figurative language, wordplay, assonance, alliteration, and, above all, meter. The meter is a matter of syllable length, so that each line is like a string of quarter notes and eighth notes arranged in a special sequence. The dialogue and speeches are written to be spoken, in iambic meter (short-long). The choral odes, the *Parodos* or Entry-song and the five stasima, are written to be sung, in a variety of complex meters, to the musical accompaniment of a drum and a reed instrument called the *aulos* (usually translated "flute"). These odes are composed of pairs of metrically identical stanzas called strophes and antistrophes. In addition, several passages for chorus, or chorus leader, are neither strophic nor iambic; for example, lines 155–62 are written to be chanted by the chorus in a rhythm of anapests (short-short-long). There are also a few strophic passages for a single voice, such as the solos for Antigone (806–82) and those for Creon (1261 to the end). (A complete layout of the verse-forms in the play is found in Griffith 1999, pp. 14–5.)

The play was staged in an open amphitheater under natural light. The chorus danced and sang in a round space known as the orchestra; the actors worked from a raised platform with two long entry ramps, one on each side. A third entrance was provided by large doors at center stage, opening into a set that represents the palace. Actors entering or leaving by the ramps could be seen by other actors and the audience before those who were entering could engage in dialogue. Only three actors were employed in a performance, and all actors were men. The actor playing Antigone might also have played Haemon and Tiresias, so that Creon's antagonists all would have had one voice, though this actor would have worn a different mask for each role.

Poets were free to give new shape to old myths. Sophocles chose to retell the old story of the unburied dead (page ix above) in personal terms. It's not the whole army of Argos that is unburied; it is only Polyneices (but see lines 1080–3). And the burial is achieved not by the whole army of Athens under Theseus, as in the old myth, but by one young woman, Antigone, who is engaged to marry the son of the king. As far as we know, Sophocles invented this variant on the myth for just this play; the resulting collisions of niece and uncle, son and father, are far more intense theatrically than the clash of armies, which could not be shown onstage. By this change, Sophocles has enabled his characters to touch our sympathies beyond what is usual in ancient Greek tragedy. They move us because they are moved by each other; each one follows a great passion, but each one shifts under our eyes as one passion enters the force field of another.

Antigone cares about her brother and worships the gods below. Creon cares about his city and the principle of hierarchy that he thinks sustains it. Haemon and Ismene are passionate about Antigone. The Watchman cares about his own life. The chorus are exuberant over Thebes' victory, Tiresias is bitterly upset at the pollution that blocks his sacred tasks, and the Messenger is grieved at the fall of the family he serves. Eurydice is said to reveal her furious anger at Creon. We are caught by these many passions, and we are tempted to share them, but we are troubled by the changes each character's passion seems to undergo.

Antigone

Antigone's name comes from the Greek for "born" and "against," and she was plainly born for trouble. She is so passionate about her cause that at the start she does not seem to care if it leads her to death in place of marriage. But Antigone's assurance gives way

to grief as she approaches death. Isolated in her new understanding that the elders of Thebes do not support her, she mourns
her own death.

The list of charges critics have made against Antigone is long.
She leaves her home in the dark before dawn to conspire with her
sister, and such activity in the dark is forbidden to women. She
takes on burial, which is men's work. In a play intended for a male
audience, she does not accept male authority, and she threatens the
order of the city by violating an order of the king. She prefers burial to marriage and a brother to a husband, perhaps because she
has an incestuous longing to lie in the embrace of her brother
beneath the ground (line 73). Aside from her devotion to her dead
brother, Antigone is harsh and unloving, cruel to Ismene, and
thoughtless of Haemon. Her justifications for burying her brother
are not consistent with each other: first an appeal to a general
unwritten law about burial, then a claim about her particular obligation to her brother. Antigone is vulnerable on both points. The
unwritten law against non-burial exists in her imagination; the concept of unwritten law was unheard of before *Antigone*, and in any
case it is legal to leave traitors unburied. Some critics have attacked
her argument from a particular relationship as having nothing to
do with serious morality—which, most modern philosophers have
agreed, must follow universal imperatives. So run the charges
against Antigone.

Many scholars have agreed with Goethe, who said that
the motive stated for Antigone in lines 904–20 is "quite unworthy of her, which almost borders on the comic." The great English scholar Sir Richard Jebb agreed that the lines were unworthy
of Sophocles; along with many scholars, he treats the lines as
spurious.

Defenders of Antigone, however, defend these difficult lines as
well (Cropp, Neuburg, Murnaghan, and others). One of the most
interesting defenses (Foley 1996) shows how Antigone's reasoning fits the particular situation in which she finds herself; her
moral reasoning is similar to that which Carol Gilligan defends
in her book, *In a Different Voice*. According to Gilligan, men in
western cultures typically prefer reasoning from general abstract
principles of the kind Creon and Haemon use, and they tend to
disregard or scorn the kind of moral reasoning that is based upon
particular relationships, which she believes is common among
women.

Perhaps some of the charges against Antigone are true, but it is surely wrong to blame her for being harsh and unloving. In ancient Greek culture, the man desires the woman, not the other way around. As Antigone is not yet married to Haemon, she has no obligation to him, aside from that of a cousin. (This alone may explain the exclamation, "O Haemon, dearest," if it is hers at line 572, which uses the expression for family-feeling, not sexual love.) As for Ismene, Antigone tries to save her life by leaving a distance between them. Although her words are harsh, we know how painful they are to Antigone (551), and her intention may be to save a life. Her love for Polyneices is, indeed, troubling in view of the incestuous history of her family; she is, after all, the daughter of her own half-brother. In this, as in other aspects of the play, we must remember that however much we may love Antigone, she belongs to a family that bears a curse. As for her decision to bury her brother, this is incumbent on her as a family member, since Creon has declined the responsibility. If she plays the part of a man, it is because no one else in the immediate family is left to do so.

The most striking features of Antigone are her unique approaches to law and to love. Antigone obeys a law that she says belongs to:

> the gods' unfailing
> Unwritten laws. These laws weren't made now
> Or yesterday. They live for all time,
> And no one knows when they came into the light. (456–9)

We do know, however, that no surviving text older than *Antigone* refers to such a concept of unwritten law. The concept probably comes into the light in the fifth century along with increasing awareness of potential conflicts between human law (*nomos*) and nature (*physis*). With these oft-quoted lines, *Antigone* inaugurates the tradition of natural law in European thought. For Hegel, the lines carry even more significance; they acknowledge "the absoluteness of the right" (see the Appendix, page 63).

For Antigone, love has mainly to do with family relationships forged at birth. Only once is a word implying erotic love associated with her, but that is when Ismene tells Antigone that she loves the impossible (line 90). Elsewhere Antigone's words for love connote the reciprocal relationship that binds family and friends together. (On Antigone's love and friendship, see Blundell 1989.) Her most famous speech about love must be read with care:

> I cannot side with hatred. My nature sides with love. (523)

Her point is that no one has enemies by birth; by nature one is tied only to family. On the whole, her love appears to be hard-headed, unsentimental, and traditional. But her longing for her brother is remarkable:

> I will have a noble death
> And lie with him, a dear sister with a dear brother. (72–3)

The verb "lie with" has sexual connotations in Greek, just as in English, and this may have sent a shock through the original audience.

Creon

Creon's name means "ruler." His devotion to rational order and even-handed justice grows darker as his suspicions of conspiracy grow: We see him looking more and more like a tyrant as the play progresses. He is not ambitious, however, and his passion is not for himself or his own power, but for the principle of hierarchy without which he thinks the city will founder, like a ship in a storm with no captain at the helm.

The dreadful threat of civil war lies upon him; when he hears that his edict against the traitor has been violated, his suspicions begin to multiply and his judgment deteriorates. He is obsessed with two ideas, both of them wrong: that the city is like a ship at sea in a storm and that the people around him are swayed by money. The ship-of-state image is a common trope, but an autocratic one, used mainly by enemies of democracy. It is true that a ship needs the firm hand of a captain and that the captain must make decisions without calling a meeting of the crew; but the democratic people of Athens felt strongly that their city needed only elected leaders, or leaders appointed by lot, who would listen to voices from the people. Creon is a very poor listener, as his son rightly points out.

Money is a red herring. None of Creon's antagonists care about money. They care about what is right and about him and his family, and some of them care about the city. But Creon's suspicions

blind him, and he misjudges one person after another—the Watchman, Ismene, Haemon, and Tiresias. His career is a living illus-
tration of power subverting good judgment.

And yet Creon does yield, unlike Antigone, who has shown
consistently the grand rigidity of her doomed father. Twice Creon
listens, though he seems to have a delayed reaction both times.
He hears the chorus's plea for Ismene and spares her life because
he has heard Antigone's plea, much earlier, to recognize Ismene's
innocence. He also heeds the chorus about Tiresias, after the seer
departs. Then Creon takes the advice he had earlier received from
Tiresias too late, of course; still, he shows that he is not an unyield-
ing tyrant. In the end, we must see that he went wrong, but we
must also pity him. Although some critics are contemptuous of
his lament, I found it quite moving. He has no reason to mourn
at length: We have heard the long dirge Antigone sings to herself,
felt the pity expressed by the Messenger, and readied ourselves
for the play to end when Creon's dead wife is wheeled through
the great doors onto the stage.

Ismene

Ismene will surprise us more than anyone else in the play. When
we first hear from her, she seems numb, unable to call up any feelings about the future, and passive in the face of events. She is
afraid to break the law, afraid of death, and unwilling to challenge
male authority:

> How horrible it will be to die outside the law,
> If we violate a dictator's decree!
> No. We have to keep this fact in mind:
> We are women and we do not fight with men. (59–62)

If women are to resist men, Ismene can imagine them doing it only
in secret (84). In this, she conforms to what men expected of
women at the time; she also takes on an attitude common people
adopt to separate themselves from the dangerous ambitions of
rulers:

> My mind
> Will never aim too high, too far. (67–8)

She conforms in other ways as well to the ancient Greek male concept of the feminine. But, in the end, she tries to share Antigone's punishment:

> But these are your troubles! I'm not ashamed;
> I'll be your shipmate in suffering. (540–1)

> No, please! You're my sister: Don't despise me!
> Let me die with you and sanctify our dead. (544–5)

Now she has forgotten her advice against resisting male authority; now she argues against Creon. Ismene is the first to mention the planned marriage between Antigone and Haemon, probably delivering the audience a surprise (568). It may also be she who breaks out with a brief, fond address to Haemon: "O Haemon, dearest" (572) in protest against Creon's attitude toward the marriage.

What has given Ismene the courage to take on Creon in this way? Perhaps it is her unswerving love for her sister, which parallels Antigone's love for Polyneices. Perhaps, also, she is reacting to Creon's rush to judgment, his unreasoning conclusion that Ismene is Antigone's accomplice (531–5).

Watchman

The Watchman is the only common man or woman to speak in this play, and he is not afraid to speak his mind—even to talk back—to Creon. In speaking his mind, he shows up the aristocratic chorus of elders, so that his voice must have delighted and amused the democratic audience of Athens. When Creon reveals how much he has been troubled by the news, the Watchman replies:

> So where's it biting you?
> On your ears or in your mind? (317)

Surely the playwright expected a laugh on this line. And elsewhere, in his outspoken concern for his own life, the Watchman is antiheroic to the point of comedy. He is, nevertheless, a man of refinement. He knows the conventions in poetry and drama for messengers, and he is clever enough to make fun of them on his first entrance:

> I can't say I am out of breath.
> I have not exactly been "running on light feet." (223–4)

His account of the arrest of Antigone is poetic, however, and charged with strong images:

> She gave a shrill cry like a bird when she sees her nest
> Empty, and the bed deserted where her nestlings had lain. (424–5)

But we should keep in mind that messengers in ancient tragedy often speak in heightened language that takes them out of character. The Watchman is here taking on the voice of a messenger; in speeches such as this, the origins of ancient drama in narrative poetry come close to the surface.

Haemon

Haemon's name carries an echo of the blood that is spilled behind the scenes in this play. He changes under our eyes from dutiful son to rebellious youth (a pattern familiar to parents of young adults). I discussed the change earlier (page xiii), but more needs to be said here about Haemon as we first know him. He is remarkably like his father. His main speech is the same length as Creon's, and, like Creon's, it is based on large generalizations about government and good judgment. Like his father, Haemon steers clear of addressing the moral issue of burial versus non-burial. He does, however, put his finger on exactly what is wrong with Creon—his rigidity and his inability to listen to opinions he does not share.

Athenian audiences would have been shocked by the sight of a son arguing with and making threats against his father; this may have been enough to turn them against the young man. But the speech Creon takes to be a threat (751) is actually a promise of suicide, and the arguments Haemon gives would have been admired, on the whole, by tyranny-hating Athenians. So the audience may have remained sympathetic to Haemon throughout this scene. The real horror—Haemon taking a sword to his father—is yet to come. Even then, he has been driven mad by the lethal combination of anger at his father's insults and grief for the woman he loves.

Tiresias

Tiresias, the blind prophet, is never wrong and almost never believed in tragic drama. In this play, for once, he is believed, but too late. Only he, aside from Antigone, dares to address non-burial.

Like Ismene and Haemon before him, he is stung to anger by Creon's suspicions and changes from a distraught diviner to a furious old man who tells a piece of the future he had planned to hold back—the death of Haemon.

Messenger

The Messenger vividly tells what cannot be shown onstage, with all the art of a storyteller. On the whole, he speaks for the poet as narrator in this play, but he has his own views and delivers his own commentary on the disaster that has fallen upon the first family of Thebes. He is the only character who is not changed by circumstances in the play.

Eurydice

Eurydice's presence is brief and to the point. She is the suffering audience for the Messenger, and she provides the perspective from which we can feel the full horror of her son's death. Her change will take place offstage when she rails at her husband and calls him "Childkiller."

The Chorus

The chorus consists of fifteen men who have been summoned by Creon to serve as his Council of Elders. As a group, they sing and dance the choral odes. Their leader, however, speaks for them when the chorus enter into dialogue with the main characters. They defer to Creon at the outset (211–4), but they show more independence of judgment as the play progresses. When they do venture to give advice to the king, he usually takes it. They influence the course of the plot by these means on two occasions: by saving Ismene from execution (770) and by persuading Creon to follow the advice of Tiresias (1091–4). But they are cautious on the whole and reluctant to take sides ("Both sides spoke well," line 725). Their attitude toward Antigone is puzzling: they think her as mad as her father, impetuous, stubborn, and wrongheaded (471–2, 853–6, 875, 929–30). But they recognize that she has chosen a path that leads to glory:

> . . . when you die, you will be great,
> You will be equal in memory to the gods,
> By the glory of your life and death. (836–8)

They admire her without taking her side, and this makes them appear weak and uncertain. The chorus are even more puzzling in the odes; each ode presents its own problems.

The *Parodos* or Entry-song (lines 100–54) is a hymn of jubilation. The ode begins by praising the sun, proceeds to recognize the power of Zeus, and ends by turning to Bacchus (Dionysus), the god of wine and dance. This shifting focus, unusual in such an ode, promises us a wild ride from the chorus and a turn to Dionysus toward the end of the play.

The First Stasimon (lines 332–75) is known as the Ode to Man. It is the most famous of Sophocles' choral poems. From the first line, the ode is ambiguous: "There are many things that are *deinos*," the Greek term meaning both "wonderful" and "terrible." Ambiguities continue to pepper the lines—for example, the word translated "character" in line 357 may also mean "anger"—and the meaning of the ode in context is uncertain. The chorus are condemning someone, but whom? Creon? Antigone? the human race? or the male gender? Why does this come now, after Creon has made his decree and had it ratified by the chorus? We are left to draw our own conclusions.

The premise of the ode comes from a theory that was new at the time Sophocles wrote: that humankind found its own means of survival without help from the gods. This humanist theory was probably taught by various sophists and philosophers of the period such as Protagoras and Democritus. (For a review of such theories, see Guthrie 1971, pp. 60–84; for the imagery of the ode, see Segal 1981.) Curiously, the chorus deliver this theory with a mixture of pride and terror. It is wonderful to count up the many things human beings have invented, but it is horrible to contemplate the effects of their inventions on the sacred earth and the wild beasts that roam upon it:

> For he is Man, and he is cunning.
> He has invented ways to take control
> Of beasts that range mountain meadows;
> Taken down the shaggy-necked horses,
> The tireless mountain bulls,
> And put them under the yoke. (347–52)

The fear of Man implicit in these lines is one a modern environmentalist could share; but it goes further, because the metaphor of putting wild beasts under the yoke bears on both political and gender relations. The yoke is a common image for marriage in ancient Greek poetry, and Creon has already used the yoke as an image for his authority as king (293). The dark turn at the end of the ode comes as a shock: Man (the gender is clear on this point) may have tamed animals and women, but he has not tamed death, and disaster awaits those who are wicked.

In the Second Stasimon (lines 582–625), the chorus sing of the power of *atê*. Now that Creon has condemned Antigone and Ismene to death, the chorus sing to this power that is both madness and the destruction that follows on madness; *atê* is sent by Zeus as a punishment to the family of Labdacus (Antigone's ancestor—see the Theban Royal Family Tree, page xxxi). While the chorus must be referring to the madness of Antigone and Ismene at one level (561–2), the Athenian audience must have felt that this was odd. They knew that Antigone was doing the right thing, exactly what Athens did in the other version of the myth, when the city sent its army to bury the Argive dead. And Athenians took great pride in this myth. So, perhaps, the madness has infected Creon, and this, at a deeper level, is the meaning of the ode. (On the ode, see Else 1976; on the pride of Athens, see Bennett and Tyrrell 1990.)

The Third Stasimon (lines 781–800) is an ode to sexual love, which may startle a modern audience unused to the ancient Greek poetic tradition of fearing love as evil. Before Plato, ancient Greece's most famous love poet, Sappho, set the tone for writers on love:

> It's love again! Limb-loosener, he makes me shake,
> The bitter-sweet, the impossible creeping thing!
> (Fragment 130, my translation)

In Sophocles' ode, the madness is apparently Haemon's; his father has plainly accused him of having been unmanned by love of a woman (746, 756). But as always, other meanings are lurking beneath the surface. Haemon's plea was to family-feeling and justice, not love (741, 743), and the character first associated in the text with love is Antigone, who loves the impossible (90) and seems to cherish an odd kind of love for her brother.

The Fourth Stasimon (lines 944–87) is beautiful and puzzling. This evocation of myths of death and premature burial is meant to provide comfort to Antigone as she is led to her death down the long ramp leading to the plain outside the city. She hears it all; it is what she has from her people in place of a marriage hymn. Creon might hear it as well; if so, his presence could dampen expressions of sympathy from the chorus.

The Fifth Stasimon (lines 1115–54) is sung at the terrifying crisis of the play. Creon has hurried off in the desperate hope of righting the wrong he has done; but now the chorus sing an ecstatic hymn to Dionysus, recapturing the mood of the *Parodos* with its final invocation. They pray for protection (1134), for healing (1143) and, most beautifully, for the blessing of dance (1146–54). They will be interrupted by the Messenger with ghastly news. So why this hymn of praise and supplication? Why now? Again, we are left to draw our own conclusions, but the beauty of the ode is itself a comfort to reader or audience at this harsh moment in the play. Keep in mind that Dionysus was believed to preside over the theatre in which this play was performed and that the final expulsion of Antigone's accursed and autocratic family will be a healing for Thebes.

The Life of Sophocles

Sophocles lived through astonishing changes during his long life (495–405 B.C.E.). As a boy, he celebrated the naval victory of the Athenians' Greek allies over the Persians at Salamis. As an adult, he served as an official at the zenith of the Athenian empire, survived the great plague, and saw the shadows closing in on Athens when their enemies, the Spartans, neared victory in the Peloponnesian War. Athenian democracy came to full flower when Sophocles was a young man. When he was in midlife, the New Learning burst upon Athens with its challenge to the old order of ideas. In old age, he saw democracy threatened and severely wounded by war and right-wing agitation.

His themes belong partly to his own time—attacks on traditional reverence by intellectuals or tyrants—and partly to all time, or at least to all human time. More than any of his contemporaries, he dwells in his poetry on the enduring question of what it is to be human in a world that does not bend itself to support human ambitions.

Sophocles was the most successful Athenian playwright of the fifth century B.C.E. He first competed in the festival of 468 and won first place against Aeschylus. Of his 120 plays, only 7 complete tragedies survive. *Oedipus at Colonus*, his last play, was written in extreme old age and brought to the stage after his death. The only other play for which we have a firm date, *Philoctetes*, was produced in 409. Otherwise, dating is uncertain, but scholars generally place *Antigone* at about 442–1 and *Oedipus Tyrannus* some time later, perhaps after the terrible plague in Athens of 430–29.

We know that the Athenians loved his work, for they awarded him twenty victories in the contest of plays. They must also have loved the man himself, because they made him a treasurer in 443 and a general, with Pericles, in 441. At the city's moment of greatest need, after the disaster of 413 in Sicily, the Athenians turned to Sophocles as one of the ten advisers empowered to see them through the crisis. After his death, they honored him as a hero, probably for his role in bringing the cult of the healer-god, Asclepius, to Athens.

PAUL WOODRUFF

Suggestions for Further Reading

Antigone has appealed to literary critics and philosophers alike; at the same time, the play has kept a great many classical scholars busy on historical and textual issues. No careful reader should be confined to an exclusive approach, whether literary, philosophical, or historical; indeed, all of the works discussed below take heed of the full range of what is known and thought about the play. Nevertheless, I have separated the three approaches for the purpose of this note. Full bibliographical details are to be found in the Selected Bibliography.

Among literary treatments, the best are those by Reinhardt (1947), Goheen (1951), and Segal (1981 and 1995). The first two do not bear the mark of recent critical theories, but both show depth and sensitivity that are immune to the ravages of time and the cycles of fashion. Charles Segal's work also must be read by anyone with a literary interest in the play. *Antigone* is the source of a wide stream of influence on modern literature, which is thoroughly discussed in Steiner (1984).

As for philosophy, Hegel used *Antigone* both to undergird his phenomenology and to illustrate his theory of tragedy; most modern studies of the play begin with his work, which concerns the conflict of the two main characters on ethical points (Paolucci 1962 below, page 63). Recently, two philosophers, Nussbaum (1986) and Blundell (1989), have studied the ethical meaning of the play in depth. Both carry the discussion beyond Hegelian theory. A valuable article by Foley (1996) brings up the gender-related issues involved in moral reasoning.

Classical scholars, especially in recent years, have studied the play in its historical context; for this they discuss ancient attitudes toward politics, law, gender, and religion. Although most of this work is published in scholarly journals, some of it deserves to be read by general readers. Griffith's superb introduction (1999) covers the entire gamut of scholarship and interpretation; Foley (1995) reviews two recent accounts of the play that are based on history.

Among translations, those of Blundell (1998) and Lloyd-Jones (1994) closely follow the Greek and reflect recent scholarly opinion; of the two, I prefer Blundell, who accepts more conservative, and more likely, readings of the text. Grene's translation (1991) is both accurate and readable. Of the literary translations, the work of Fagles (1982) rightly enjoys a high reputation.

Readers with a little Greek should consult the new commentary by Griffith (1999) and the elegant classic by Jebb (1900) on all points.

Note on the Translation

In these lines, I have tried to capture the dramatic and poetic intensity of the ancient Greek play without sacrificing accuracy. Any success I have had in producing a stageable version is due to what I learned from Peter Meineck through our work on *Oedipus Tyrannus* and through my studying his *Oedipus at Colonus*; his influence is felt in almost every line. I am grateful also to James Collins for extensive help with both the Selected Bibliography and the Introduction (especially on understanding Hegel) and to Brian Rak for editorial suggestions.

Line numbers refer to the Greek text, which I have translated line for line except for a few instances. I have provided stage directions that reflect ancient theatrical productions. We do not always know for certain which character gives each speech. When there is more than one possibility, I give all of them at the head of the speech.

Footnotes explain words and ideas necessary for a basic understanding of the text and warn readers about alternative readings that yield different meanings from those I have rendered. A note on the text, with endnotes about textual issues, follows the translation.

Theban Royal Family Tree

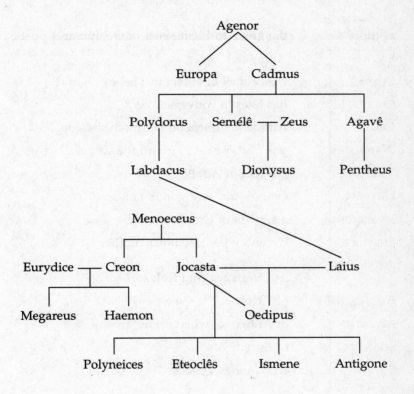

Cast of Characters

ANTIGONE   daughter and half-sister of Oedipus

ISMENE   Antigone's sister

CHORUS   the council of elders in Thebes

CHORUS LEADER   has lines in conversations

CREON   Antigone's uncle on her mother's side

WATCHMAN   one of those set to guard the corpse

TIRESIAS   prophet of Apollo

HAEMON   Creon's son, Antigone's fiancé

MESSENGER   a servant of Creon's

EURYDICE   Creon's wife, Haemon's mother

Nonspeaking Roles

ATTENDANTS   of Creon

ATTENDANTS   of Antigone (when under arrest)

SERVANTS   of Eurydice

BOY   who guides Tiresias

Antigone

SCENE: *The royal house at Thebes, fronting onto a raised*
platform stage. Wing entrances right and left allow for
characters to be seen by the audience and the chorus
long before they are seen by the main characters. The
great doors of the house stand upstage center.

(Enter Antigone leading Ismene through the great
doors that lead from the palace.)

ANTIGONE:
    Ismene, dear heart, my true sister:
    You and I are left alive to pay
    The final penalty to Zeus for Oedipus.
    I've never seen such misery and madness—
    It's monstrous! Such deep shame and dishonor—   5
    As this, which falls upon the pair of us.
    And now, a public announcement!
    They say the general has plastered it around the city.
    Have you heard this terrible news or not?
    Our enemies are on the march to hurt our friends.   10

ISMENE:
    No, Antigone, I have had no news of friends,
    Nothing sweet or painful, since the day
    We lost our brothers, both of us, on one day,
    Both brothers dead by their two hands.
    Last night the army that came from Argos   15

10: By "friends" Antigone means her brother Polyneices, who is her
friend, come what may, because he is part of her immediate family. But
who are her enemies? As I understand her, Antigone is revealing that she
has already identified Creon as the enemy. See endnote for alternative
readings.

14–15: The two brothers, Eteoclês and Polyneices, had planned to take
turns ruling Thebes; but Eteoclês refused to give Polyneices his time on
the throne. An army came from Argos in support of Polyneices' claim and

1

Disappeared, and after that I don't know
Anything that could bring me happiness—or despair.

ANTIGONE:
I knew it! That's the whole reason
I brought you outside—to hear the news alone.

ISMENE:
20   Tell me. You're as clear as a fog at sea.

ANTIGONE:
It's the burial of our two brothers. Creon
Promotes one of them and shames the other.
Eteoclês—I heard Creon covered him beneath
The earth with proper rites, as law ordains,
25   So he has honor down among the dead.
But Polyneices' miserable corpse—
They say Creon has proclaimed to everyone:
"No Burial of any kind. No wailing, no public tears.
Give him to the vultures, unwept, unburied,
30   To be a sweet treasure for their sharp eyes and beaks."
That's what they say the good Creon has proclaimed
To you. And me. He forbids me, too.
And now he's strutting here to make it plain
To those who haven't heard—he takes
35   This seriously—that if anyone does what he forbids
He'll have him publicly stoned to death.
There's your news. Now, show your colors:
Are you true to your birth? Or a coward?

ISMENE:
You take things hard. If we are in this noose,
40   What could I do to loosen or pull tight the knot?

ANTIGONE:
If you share the work and trouble . . .

---

was defeated at the seven gates of the city. The two brothers killed each
other. Argos, in the northeast corner of Peloponnesus, was seen as an
enemy of Thebes.

21: "Creon"—In her breathless haste, Antigone frequently starts a
thought just before the end of a line.

25: See Introduction, p. x on burial rites.

ISMENE:
    In what dangerous adventure?

ANTIGONE:
    If you help this hand raise the corpse . . . *(Indicating her
        own hand)*

ISMENE:
    Do you mean to bury him? Against the city's ordinance?

ANTIGONE:
    But he is mine. And yours. Like it or not, he's our brother.   45
    They'll never catch me betraying him.

ISMENE:
    How horrible! When Creon forbids it?

ANTIGONE:
    He has no right to keep me from my own.

ISMENE:
    Oh no! Think carefully, my sister.
    Our father died in hatred and disgrace   50
    After gouging out his own two eyes
    For sins he'd seen in his own self.
    Next, his mother and wife—she was both—
    Destroyed herself in a knotted rope.
    And, third, our two brothers on one day   55
    Killed each other in a terrible calamity,
    Which they had created for each other.
    Now think about the two of us. We are alone.
    How horrible it will be to die outside the law,
    If we violate a dictator's decree!   60
    No. We have to keep this fact in mind:
    We are women and we do not fight with men.
    We're subject to them because they're stronger,
    And we must obey this order, even if it hurts us more.
    As for me, I will say to those beneath the earth   65
    This prayer: "Forgive me, I am held back by force."
    And I'll obey the men in charge. My mind
    Will never aim too high, too far.

ANTIGONE:
    I won't press you any further. I wouldn't even let
    You help me if you had a change of heart.   70

Go on and *be* the way you choose to be. I
Will bury him. I will have a noble death
And lie with him, a dear sister with a dear brother.
Call it a crime of reverence, but I must be good to those
75   Who are below. I will be there longer than with you.
That's where I will lie. You, keep to your choice:
Go on insulting what the gods hold dear.

ISMENE:
I am not insulting anyone. By my very nature
I cannot possibly take arms against the city.

ANTIGONE:
80   Go on, make excuses. I am on my way.
I'll heap the earth upon my dearest brother's grave.

ISMENE:
Oh no! This is horrible for you. I am so worried!

ANTIGONE:
Don't worry about me. Put your own life straight.

ISMENE:
Please don't tell a soul what you are doing.
85   Keep it hidden. I'll do the same.

ANTIGONE:
For god's sake, speak out. You'll be more enemy to me
If you are silent. Proclaim it to the world!

ISMENE:
Your heart's so hot to do this chilling thing!

ANTIGONE:
But it pleases those who matter most.

ISMENE:
90   Yes, if you had the power. But you love the impossible.

ANTIGONE:
So? When my strength is gone, I'll stop.

89: "Those who matter most"—the dead, or the gods of the dead.

90: "You love the impossible"—more accurately, perhaps, "You long for
the impossible." But the verb is the same as the one used for sexual love.
On Antigone's love, see Introduction, p. xviii.

ISMENE:
But it's the highest wrong to chase after what's impossible.

ANTIGONE:
When you say this, you set yourself against me.
Your brother will take you to him—as his enemy.
So you just let me and my 'bad judgment'   95
Go to hell. Nothing could happen to me
That's half as bad as dying a coward's death.

> *(Exit Antigone toward the plain, through the stage
> left wing.)*

ISMENE:
Then follow your judgment, go. You've lost your mind,
But you are holding to the love of your loved ones.

> *(Exit Ismene through the great doors into the palace,
> as the chorus enter from the city, stage right wing.)*

CHORUS:

Parodos (Entry-song)

[Strophe *a*]

Let us praise the Sun: 100
These brilliant beams
Shine glory never seen before in Thebes,
Our City of Seven Gates.
O bright eye of golden day!
You came striding over River Dirkê,   105
And the White Shield of Argos ran away.
He has fled,
Man and weapon racing from your light,
On sharpened spur.

He was roused against our land   110

100: "Let us praise the Sun"—See Introduction, p. xxiv on this choral
passage.
105: Dirkê is one of the rivers of Thebes.
106: "White Shield of Argos"—the army of Argos.

For a fight that Polyneices, haggling, picked.
And, like a screaming eagle,
He dropped on our land:
The shadow of his white-snow wing—
115   A multitude of armored men,
Helmets crested with horsehair.

[Antistrophe *a*]

He stooped over our homes,
Mouth gaping wide for the kill,
He engulfed our Seven Gates with spears of death;
120   But he has gone,
Gone before plunging his beak in our blood,
Gone before torching our crown of towers
With the flames of Hephaestus.
For behind his back there arose too loud
125   The clamor of war;
His dragon-foe was too strong for him.

Zeus hates an arrogant boast,
With towering hatred.
He saw the river of men attack,
130   Their golden armor clashing in contempt,
And so he struck the man down with a missile of fire
As he swooped toward his highest goal,
Eager to shout "Victory!"

[Strophe *b*]

He crashed to the ground
135   Like a weight slung down in an arc of fire,
This man who had swooped like a dancer in ecstasy,
Breathing hurricanes of hatred.

111: Polyneices—The chorus pun on the meaning of the young man's name, "much-quarreling."

126: "Dragon-foe"—The people of Thebes believed that they were descended from men who grew from the teeth of a dragon slain by Cadmus.

131–40: These lines refer to the attacker who boasts too much; according to the legend, this was an Argive named Kapaneus.

But his threats came to nothing:
The mighty war god, fighting beside us,
Swept them aside.   140

Seven captains at seven gates,
Matched with seven defenders,
All left trophies for Zeus the protector
(They took off their armor and ran).
Except for a savage pair, full brothers: 145
Their two spears stand upright, conquering,
Each in the other's dead breast.

                [Antistrophe *b*]

Now Victory is ours,
Great be her name! Now Thebes rejoices.
Therefore let us forget our pain.   150
The war is over: let us dance all night,
Fill all the sacred precincts with joy:
We must now be ruled by Bacchus,
Dance-master of Thebes.

        (Enter Creon through the great doors.)

CHORUS:
Here is the king of our land   155
Creon, the son of Menoeceus,
Our new ruler given us by chance and the gods.
What plan has he been churning over on his way?
Why has he summoned us—
The council of elders—   160
By public announcement?

CREON:
Gentlemen, the city is safe again, we may thank the gods:
After a great upheaval, they have rescued Thebes.
You are here because I chose you from the whole crowd

156: "Creon, the son of Menoeceus"—See Theban Royal Family Tree,
p. xxxi.
157: "Our new ruler"—Creon is not altogether new, since he was the
regent for Oedipus' sons. See line 289 with note.

165   And summoned you by escort. You always showed
            respect
        For Laius' power when he held the throne,
        And the same again for Oedipus, when he rescued Thebes.
        After he died I know you stood by their sons;
        You were always there with good advice.
170   Now they are dead, both on one day;
        Each stabbed the other and was stabbed.
        Brother struck brother, and the blows were cursed.

        So now the throne and all the power in Thebes are mine,
        Because I am closest kin to those who died.

175   No man has a mind that can be fully known,
        In character or judgment, till he rules and makes law;
        Only then can he be tested in the public eye.
        I believe that if anyone tries to run a city
        On the basis of bad policies and holds his tongue
180   Because he's afraid to say what is right,
        That man is terrible. So I have always thought.
        But it's even worse when he plays favorites,
        Puts family or friends ahead of fatherland.
        As for me—I call to witness all-seeing Zeus—
185   I will never hold my tongue about what I see
        When ruin is afoot or the city is not safe.
        I will never call a man my friend
        If he is hostile to this land. I know this well:
        The city is our lifeboat: we have no friends at all
190   Unless we keep her sailing right side up.
        Such are my laws. By them I'll raise this city high.

        And I have just announced a twin sister of those laws,
        To all the citizens, concerning Oedipus' sons:

165: "You always showed respect"—The same word covers "reverence"
and is used with that broader sense elsewhere in the play. See lines 744–5
with note.

168: "You stood by their sons"—The plural "their" in the Greek is start-
ling. We do not know whether it refers to Oedipus and Laius or to Oedipus and Jocasta. See endnote.

175–6: Cf. Aristotle, *Nicomachean Ethics* 5.1, "Ruling shows what a man is."

Eteoclês fought for the city, and for it he died,
After every feat of heroism with his spear.   195
He shall be sanctified by every burial rite
That is given to the most heroic dead below.

As for his blood brother, Polyneices by name,
He broke his exile, he came back hungry for our blood,
He wanted to burn his fatherland and family gods   200
Down from the top. He wanted to lead his people—
Into slavery. This man will have no grave:
It is forbidden to offer any funeral rites;
No one in Thebes may bury him or mourn for him.
He must be left unburied. May birds and dogs   205
Feed on his limbs, a spectacle of utter shame.

Such is the character of my mind: Never, while I rule,
Will a criminal be honored higher than a man of justice.
But give me a true friend of this city
And I will pay him full honor, in death or life.   210

CHORUS:
That is your decision, son of Menoeceus,
As to the one who meant our city well
And the one who meant it ill. It's up to you:
Make any law you want—for the dead, or for us who live.

CREON:
Now, look after my commands. I insist.   215

CHORUS:
Ask someone younger to take up the task.

CREON:
No, no. I have men already watching the corpse.

CHORUS:
Then what's left for us to do? What are your orders?

CREON:
That you do not side with anyone who disobeys.

215–6: Creon meant "see that my commands are obeyed," but the chorus understood "watch over the corpse."

CHORUS:
220   No one is foolish enough to ask for death.

CREON:
       Right. That would be their reward. But hope—
       And bribery—often have led men to destruction.

       (Enter Watchman from the stage left wing.)

WATCHMAN:
       Sir, I am here. I can't say I am out of breath.
       I have not exactly been "running on light feet."
225   I halted many times along the road so I could think,
       And I almost turned around and marched right back.
       My mind kept talking to me. It said, "You poor guy,
       Why are you going there? You'll just get your ass kicked."
       Then it said, "Are you stopping again, you damn fool?
230   If Creon hears this from another man, he'll give you hell."
       Well, I turned this idea up and down like that,
       And I hurried along, real slow. Made a short trip long.
       What got me here in the end was this: My report.
       It doesn't amount to much, but I might as well give it,
235   Because I won't let go this handful of hope
       That things won't be any worse than they have to be.

CREON:
       What is it, man—where's your courage?

WATCHMAN:
       First, I want to tell you where I stand:
       I didn't do this thing, and I don't know who did,
240   And it wouldn't be fair if I got hurt.

CREON:
       All right, your defense perimeter is up.
       Now, let's have your report.

WATCHMAN:
       It's terrible news. I can't come right out with that.

224: "Running on light feet"—An audience would normally expect a
messenger to arrive gasping and out of breath. This one consciously
flouts convention. The passage corroborates Haemon's claim, line 690 and
following, that people are afraid to tell the truth to Creon.

CREON:
  Speak up! And then get lost.

WATCHMAN:
  OK, here it is. The body out there—someone buried it   245
  Just now and went away. They spread thirsty dust
  All over the skin and did the ceremony in full.

CREON:
  What? No man would dare! Who did it?

WATCHMAN:
  I don't know. The ground was so hard and dry.
  It showed no marks. No spade scratches,   250
  No pickaxe holes, not even chariot ruts.
  The perpetrator had not left a single clue.
  When the first day-watchman showed it to us,
  We were all amazed. It was incredible:
  The guy had vanished. There was no tomb,   255
  Only fine dust lying over the body, enough to take
  The curse away. No sign of wild animals,
  No dogs sniffing or tugging at the corpse.

  We burst out shouting at each other;
  Everyone was hurling accusations.   260
  We kept coming to blows, no one to stop us.
  Any one of us could have done the thing.
  No one caught red-handed, everyone pled ignorance.
  We were about to test each other with red-hot iron
  Or run our hands through fire and swear by all the gods: 265
  "I didn't do it, and I had no part in any plot
  To do it, not with anyone else, not by hand or word."
  Well, we weren't getting anywhere, and in the end
  Someone told us to do a thing we couldn't see how
  To refuse *or* accept. So we dropped heads, stared at the
      ground   270
  In fear. There was no way it would turn out good for us.
  We simply had to bring word to you,
  Because we could not hide a thing like this.

255: "The guy had vanished"—The subject of this sentence probably is
the corpse of Polyneices.

We voted to do it, and I am so damned unlucky
275   I won the lottery to have this lovely job.
I didn't want to come. And you sure didn't want to see me:
No one loves the man who brings bad news.

CHORUS: *(To Creon.)*
You know, sir, as soon as I heard, it came to me:
Somehow the gods are behind this piece of work.

CREON: *(To the chorus leader.)*
280   Stop right there, before I'm gorged with rage!
You want to prove that you're as stupid as you are old?
It's totally unacceptable, what you said about the gods—
That they could have a caring thought for this man's corpse.
You think they buried him for his good deeds?
285   To give him highest honor? They know he came with fire
To burn down their fine-columned shrines, their land,
Their store of treasure—and to blow their laws away.
Have you ever seen a criminal honored by the *gods*?
Not possible.

But some *men* here have always champed,
290   Like surf, against my orders, and obeyed me, if at all,
Without cheer. They shake their heads when I'm not
          looking,
Pull out of the yoke of justice, and are not content with me.
They are the ones, I'm absolutely sure, who used bribes
To lead our watchmen astray, into this crime.

295   Money is the nastiest weed ever to sprout
In human soil. Money will ravage a city,
Tear men from their homes and send them into exile.
Money teaches good minds to go bad;
It is the source of every shameful human deed.
300   Money points the way to wickedness,

289: "Some *men* here have always champed"—The line suggests that Creon has been ruling for a long time. See line 157, with notes, and Introduction, p. xix.

292: "The yoke of justice"—With this powerful and undemocratic image, Creon speaks of holding his citizens to justice as he would of breaking animals to the yoke.

Lets people know the full range of irreverence.
But those who committed this crime for hire
Have set themselves a penalty, which, in time, they'll pay.

(To the Watchman.)

Now listen here. So long as I am reverent to Zeus
I am under oath, and you can be absolutely sure   305
That if you don't find the hand behind this burial
And bring him so I can see him with my own eyes,
Death alone will not be good enough for you—
Not till I've stretched you with ropes and you confess
To this outrageous crime. That will teach you   310
Where to look to make a profit. And you will learn:
Never accept money from just anyone who comes along.
Those who take from a source that is wicked, you'll see,
Are ruined far more often than saved.

WATCHMAN:
Permission to speak, sir? Or about face and go?   315

CREON:
Don't you see how badly your report annoyed me?

WATCHMAN:
So where's it biting you? On your ears or in your mind?

CREON:
What's it to you? Why should you analyze my pain?

WATCHMAN:
If it hurts your mind, blame the perpetrator.
If it's only your ears, blame me.

CREON:
Damn it, man, will you never stop babbling?   320

WATCHMAN:
Well, at least I never did the thing.

CREON:
Yes, you did. And for money! You gave up your life!

WATCHMAN:
Oh no, no, no.
It's terrible when false judgment guides the judge.

CREON:
>   All right, play with the word 'judgment.' But you'd better
>   catch
325 The man who did this thing or I'll have proof:
>   You men ruined your miserable lives to make a profit!

>   *(Creon turns and exits through the great doors to
>   the palace.)*

WATCHMAN:
>   We'll find him. You'd better believe it.
>   But if we don't—you know, if he gets lucky—
>   No way you'll ever see me coming back to you.
330 As it is, this has gone better than I expected—
>   I'm still alive, thanks be to the gods.

>   *(Exit Watchman toward the plain, through the stage
>   left wing.)*

First Stasimon

CHORUS:

[Strophe *a*]

>   Many wonders, many terrors,
>   But none more wonderful than the human race
>   Or more dangerous.
335 This creature travels on a winter gale
>   Across the silver sea,
>   Shadowed by high-surging waves,
>   While on Earth, grandest of the gods,
>   He grinds the deathless, tireless land away,

332–75: First Stasimon—See Introduction, p. xxiv.

332: "Many wonders, many terrors" (*polla ta deina*)—A word-for-word translation would be "Many things are wonderful-terrible, but none is more so than a human being." The word *deinon* is used of things that are awe-inspiring in both good and bad ways. I have rendered this double meaning by using "wonder," "terror," and "dangerous" in the opening lines.

339: "Grinds the . . . land away"—The Greek verb implies that he does this for his benefit.

Turning and turning the plow   340
From year to year, behind driven horses.

[Antistrophe *a*]

Light-headed birds he catches
And takes them away in legions. Wild beasts
    Also fall prey to him.
And all that is born to live beneath the sea   345
Is thrashing in his woven nets.
For he is Man, and he is cunning.
He has invented ways to take control
Of beasts that range mountain meadows:
Taken down the shaggy-necked horses,   350
The tireless mountain bulls,
And put them under the yoke.

[Strophe *b*]

Language and a mind swift as the wind
    For making plans—   355
These he has taught himself—
And the character to live in cities under law.
He's learned to take cover from a frost
And escape sharp arrows of sleet.
He has the means to handle every need,   360
Never steps toward the future without the means.

347: "Man"—The ode begins at line 333 with the generic "human," but
here the male of the species is plainly indicated. The quarrel between a
man and a woman that lies at the heart of the play is in the background;
Greek men of this period frequently used images of taming and con-
trolling animals for the relation between the sexes.

348: "Ways to take control"—The Greek word is used for conquest or
the illegitimate rule of a tyrant.

352: "Yoke"—This word too is politically charged. See line 292 with note.

357: "The character to live in cities"—Literally, the untranslated phrase
indicates the emotions that give order to cities. Probably the line refers
to such virtues as reverence, justice, and a sense of shame, all of which
civic life was widely thought to depend upon. See Plato's *Protagoras*
322c–d. But the word translated "character" can also mean "anger," as at
line 875.

Except for Death: He's got himself no relief from that,
Though he puts every mind to seeking cures
For plagues that are hopeless.

[Antistrophe *b*]

365   He has cunning contrivance,
            Skill surpassing hope,
        And so he slithers into wickedness sometimes,
        Other times into doing good.
        If he honors the law of the land
370   And the oath-bound justice of the gods,
        Then his city shall stand high.
        But no city for him if he turns shameless out of daring.
        He will be no guest of mine,
        He will never share my thoughts,
375   If he goes wrong.

        (*Enter Watchman leading Antigone through the
        stage left wing.*)

CHORUS:
        Monstrous! What does this mean?
        Are gods behind it? I don't know what to think:
        Isn't this Antigone? I can't deny it.
        You miserable child of misery,
380   Daughter of Oedipus,
        What have you done?
        Is it you they arrested?
        Are you so foolish?
        So disloyal to the laws of kings?

WATCHMAN:
        Yes, she's the one that did the burial.
385   We caught her in the act. Hey, where's Creon?

        (*Enter Creon through the great doors.*)

CHORUS:
        Here he is. Coming back from the palace.

376: "Monstrous"—The word refers to anything so foreign to common
experience that it may be taken as a special omen from the gods.

CREON:
  What's all this? Lucky I turned up now.

WATCHMAN:
  Sir, there's no point swearing oaths if you're a mortal.
  Second thoughts make any plan look bad.
  I swore I'd never come to you again   390
  Because those threats of yours gave me the shakes.
  But you know: "Joy beyond hope
  Surpasses every other pleasure."
  I've come, though I swore on oath I wouldn't.
  And I've brought this girl, arrested her at the grave   395
  When she was tidying it up. No lottery this time.
  The windfall's mine and no one else's.
  Now it's up to you. Take her, question her,
  Make your judgment. As for me,
  The right thing is to let me off scot-free.   400

CREON:
  Circumstances under which you arrested her? Location?

WATCHMAN:
  She was burying that man. Now you know it all.

CREON:
  Do you honestly know what you are saying?

WATCHMAN:
  Well, I saw this girl burying the dead body.
  The one you put off-limits. Clear enough for you?   405

CREON:
  How did you see this? Caught her in the act?

WATCHMAN:
  It was like this. We went back to the body
  After all your terrible threats,
  And we brushed off the dust that covered it,
  So as to make the rotting corpse properly naked.   410
  Then we settled down on the hill,
  Upwind, so the stink wouldn't hit us.
  We kept awake by yelling insults
  At each other when a slacker nodded off.
  That went on for a long time, till the sun   415

Stood bright in the center of the sky.
And we were really getting cooked. Then,
Suddenly, a tornado struck. It raised dust
All over the plain, grief to high heaven.
420   It thrashed the low-lying woods with terror
And filled the whole wide sky. We shut our eyes
And held out against this plague from the gods.

After a long while it lifted, and then we saw the girl.
She gave a shrill cry like a bird when she sees her nest
425   Empty, and the bed deserted where her nestlings had lain.
That was how she was when she saw the corpse uncovered.
She cried out in mourning, and she called down
Curses on whoever had done this thing.
Right away she spread thirsty dust with her hands,
430   Then poured the three libations from a vessel of fine bronze.
And so she crowned the corpse with honor.

As soon as we spotted her, we started to run.
She showed no fear; it was easy to catch her.
Then we questioned her about her past and present actions.
435   She did not deny a single thing.
For me, that was sweet, and agonizing, too.
It's a great joy to be out of trouble,
But bringing trouble on your friends is agony.
Still I don't mind that so much. It's nature's way
440   For me to put my own survival first.

CREON:
You there! With your head bowed to the ground—
Are you guilty? Or do you deny that you did this thing?

ANTIGONE:
Of course not. I did it. I won't deny anything.

CREON: *(To the Watchman.)*
You're dismissed. Take yourself where you please;
445   You're a free man, no serious charge against you.

419: "Grief to high heaven"—The phrase may mean "high as the sky."
430: The libations, pouring wine from a ceremonial vessel, form an essential part of ancient Greek burial ritual.

(To Antigone.)

As for you, tell me—in brief, not at length—
Did you know that this had been forbidden?

ANTIGONE:
I knew. I couldn't help knowing. It was everywhere.

CREON:
And yet you dared to violate these laws?

ANTIGONE:
What laws? I never heard it was Zeus   450
Who made that announcement.
And it wasn't justice, either. The gods below
Didn't lay down this law for human use.
And I never thought your announcements
Could give you—a mere human being—   455
Power to trample the gods' unfailing,
Unwritten laws. These laws weren't made now
Or yesterday. They live for all time,
And no one knows when they came into the light.
No man could frighten me into taking on
The gods' penalty for breaking such a law.   460
I'll die in any case, of course I will,
Whether you announce my execution or not.
But if I die young, all the better:
People who live in misery like mine
Are better dead. So if that's the way   465
My life will end, the pain is nothing.
But if I let the corpse—my mother's son—
Lie dead, unburied, that would be agony.
This way, no agony for me. But you! You think
I've been a fool? It takes a fool to think that.   470

CHORUS:
Now we see the girl's as wild by birth as her father.
She has no idea how to bow her head to trouble.

CREON: *(To the chorus.)*
Don't forget: The mind that is most rigid

473: Creon apparently does not think it worth his while to answer
Antigone; instead, he responds to the chorus in a speech that consists

Stumbles soonest; the hardest iron—
475 Tempered in fire till it is super-strong—
Shatters easily and clatters into shards.
And you can surely break the wildest horse
With a tiny bridle. When the master's watching,
Pride has no place in the life of a slave.
480 This girl was a complete expert in arrogance
Already, when she broke established law.
And now, arrogantly, she adds insult to injury:
She's boasting and sneering about what she's done!
Listen, if she's not punished for taking the upper hand,
485 Then I am not a man. *She* would be a man!
I don't care if she is my sister's child—
Or closer yet at my household shrine for Zeus—
She and her sister must pay the full price
And die for their crime.

> (*The chorus indicate their surprise that both
> must die.*)

                                    Yes, I say they have equal guilt,
490 Conniving, one with the other, for this burial.

Bring her out. I saw her in there a minute ago;
She was raving mad, totally out of her mind.
Often it's the feelings of a thief that give him away
Before the crimes he did in darkness come to light.

> (*Turning to Antigone.*)

495 But how I hate it when she's caught in the act,
And the criminal still glories in her crime.

ANTIGONE:
You've caught me, you can kill me. What more do you want?

---

mainly of a ringing list of clichés about the risks attending arrogance and
inflexible judgment—risks he is unconsciously taking himself. His opening image of hard, fragile iron prefigures Haemon's mention of stiff trees
breaking in a flood, lines 712–4.

480–2: "Arrogance . . . injury"—The Greek word hubris includes the
meanings of arrogance, insolence, outrage, and crime. Typically violating justice and reverence, hubris is practiced by the strong against the
weak.

CREON:
  For me, that's everything. I want no more than that.

ANTIGONE:
  Then what are you waiting for? More talk?
  Your words disgust me, I hope they always will.   500
  And I'm sure you are disgusted by what I say.
  But yet, speaking of glory, what could be more
  Glorious than giving my true brother his burial?
  All these men would tell you they're rejoicing
  Over that, if you hadn't locked their tongues   505
  With fear. But a tyrant says and does
  What he pleases. That's his great joy.

CREON:
  You are the only one, in all Thebes, who thinks that way.

ANTIGONE:
  No. They all see it the same. You've silenced them.

CREON:
  Aren't you ashamed to have a mind apart from theirs?   510

ANTIGONE:
  There's no shame in having respect for a brother.

CREON:
  Wasn't he your brother, too, the one who died on the
    other side?

ANTIGONE:
  Yes, my blood brother—same mother, same father.

CREON:
  When you honor the one, you disgrace the other. Why do it?

ANTIGONE:
  The dead will never testify against a burial.   515

CREON:
  Yes, if they were equal. But one of them deserves disgrace.

500: "Your words disgust me"—Although the literal translation is closer
to "are not pleasing to me," ancient Greek understatements often imply
powerful sentiments.

ANTIGONE:
He wasn't any kind of slave. He was his brother, who died.

CREON:
He was killing and plundering. The other one defended
our land.

ANTIGONE:
Even so, Hades longs to have these laws obeyed.

CREON:
520   But surely not equal treatment for good and bad?

ANTIGONE:
Who knows? Down below that might be blesséd.

CREON:
An enemy is always an enemy, even in death.

ANTIGONE:
I cannot side with hatred. My nature sides with love.

CREON:
Go to Hades, then, and if you have to love, love someone
dead.
525   As long as I live, I will not be ruled by a woman.

(Enter Ismene under guard, through the great doors.)

CHORUS:
Now Ismene stands before the doors
And sheds tears of sister-love.

519: Hades is the god of death, his name is also used for the Underworld,
to which the dead belong. See Introduction, p. x.

523: "I cannot side with hatred. My nature sides with love"—Antigone
coins new words here for her extraordinary feelings. She means that
even if her brothers hate each other, it is her nature not to join them in
hatred, but in the family love (*philia*) they have for her. Note also that
family love is natural, i.e., by birth, unlike any sort of enmity: "I have
friends by birth, not enemies" (Lloyd-Jones 1994). See Introduction,
p. xviii on Antigone's love.

527–30: Because the actor is wearing a mask, Ismene's expression must
be described. What shows on her face is important because Creon takes
it as a sign of guilt.

From her brows, a blood-dark cloud
Casts a foul shadow
And stains her lovely face.   530

CREON:
Now you. Hiding in my house like a snake,
A coiled bloodsucker in the dark! And I never realized
I was raising a pair of deadly, crazed revolutionaries!
Come, tell me: How do you plead? Guilty of this burial
As an accomplice? Or do you swear you knew nothing?   535

ISMENE:
I did it, I confess. That is, if we are partners, anyway.
I am an accomplice, and I bear responsibility with her.

ANTIGONE:
I will not permit this penalty to fall on you.
No. I never wanted to give you a share.

ISMENE:
But these are your troubles! I'm not ashamed;   540
I'll be your shipmate in suffering.

ANTIGONE:
I have witnesses: the gods below saw who did the work.
I won't accept a friend who's only friends in words.

ISMENE:
No, please! You're my sister: Don't despise me!
Let me die with you and sanctify our dead.   545

ANTIGONE:
No, you may not die along with me. Don't say you did it!
You wouldn't even touch it. Now leave my death alone!

ISMENE:
Why would I care to live when you are gone?

ANTIGONE:
Creon's the one to ask. He's the one you care for.

ISMENE:
Why are you scolding me? It won't help you.   550

538–9: Cf. lines 69–70.

ANTIGONE:
Of course not. It hurts me when my mockery strikes you.

ISMENE:
But I still want to help you. What can I do?

ANTIGONE:
Escape! Save yourself! I don't begrudge you that.

ISMENE:
O misery! Why am I cut off from your fate?

ANTIGONE:
555   Because you chose life, and I chose death.

ISMENE:
But I gave you reasons not to make that choice.

Antigone: *(Pointing to Creon and the chorus.)*
Oh yes, you are sensible; these men agree.

> *(Pointing to the ground, speaking of the dead or the gods below.)*

But *they* agree with me.

ISMENE:
Yes, I know. And now the sin is mine as much as yours.

ANTIGONE:
Be brave. You are alive. Already my soul is dead.
560   It has gone to help those who died before me.

CREON:
What a pair of children! One of you lost her mind
Moments ago; the other was born without hers.

ISMENE:
That is right, sir. Whenever we commit a crime,
Our minds, which grew by nature, leave us.

CREON:
565   Yours did, when you deliberately joined a criminal in crime.

ISMENE:
Without her, why should I live? I'd be alone.

555: Cf. lines 71–81.

CREON:
  Her? Don't speak of her. She is no more.

ISMENE:
  But will you really kill the bride of your son?

CREON:
  There's other ground for him to plow, you know.

ISMENE:
  But no one is suited to him as well as she is.   570

CREON:
  I loathe bad women. She's not for my son.

ANTIGONE (or possibly ISMENE, or possibly CHORUS):
  O Haemon, dearest, what a disgrace your father does to you!

CREON:
  Shut up! What a pain you are, you and your marriage!

CHORUS (or ISMENE, or ANTIGONE):
  Will you really take away your son's bride?

CREON:
  Not me. Death will put a stop to this marriage.   575

CHORUS (or ISMENE):
  So she will die. Has it really been decided?

CREON:
  Yes. By you and me. Now, no more delays.

572: The old manuscripts do not reliably tell us which character speaks
which lines. In this case, modern editors are divided. Some think that
Ismene speaks throughout the scene; others assign this line to Antigone.
Sophocles does not elsewhere change speakers in mid-conversation; but
in 573, Creon is more likely to be responding to Antigone than to Ismene,
and in 577 he cannot be replying to Ismene. So the conversation is bro-
ken in any event. Besides, if any tragic character would break into a conversation, it would be Antigone.

   The line does not imply sentimental love for Haemon so much as family-feeling; he is after all the sisters' cousin. On Antigone's love, see Introduction, p. xviii.

574, 576: Some editors assign these lines to Ismene, some to the chorus,
and some to Antigone.

577: "By you and me"—Who has joined Creon in condemning Antigone

Servants! Take them inside. They are women,
And they must not be free to roam about.
580   Even a brave man flees from Death
When he sees his life in immediate danger.

> (Servants take Ismene and Antigone through the
> great doors.)

Second Stasimon

CHORUS:

[Strophe *a*]

Happy are they that never taste of crime,
But once a house is shaken by the gods,
Then madness stalks the family without fail,
585   Disaster for many generations.
It is like a great salt wave
Kicked up by foul winds from Thrace,
It surges over the hellish depths of the sea,
Roils the bottom,
590   Churns up black sand,
And makes the screaming headlands howl
Against the gale.

---

to death? Not Ismene. The chorus support the decree at 211–4, and Antigone seems to accept her fate at 461–6; in a sense she has condemned herself by her actions. But only the elders of the chorus have the standing to ratify the ruler's decision.

582–625: Second Stasimon—Creon, who is present throughout the ode, must assume that the chorus are singing about the ruin of Antigone and, consequently, of the house of Oedipus; but the chorus may have the entire royal family in mind, including Creon's branch of it. See Introduction, p. xxv, and Else (1976) on the charge of madness against Antigone.

582: "Happy are they that never taste of crime"—The word translated as "crime" could mean simply "trouble," but line 622 shows that the chorus are thinking of serious wrongdoing.

584–5: "Madness . . . disaster"—*atê.* The ode revolves around the double meaning of this one word—blindness or madness on the one hand, ruin or destruction on the other. In lines 614 and 625, I have rendered it "disaster."

[Antistrophe *a*]

I see grief falling from old days on Labdacus' family:
New grief heaped on the grief of those who died.
And nothing redeems the generation that is to come: 595
Some god is battering them without relief.
Now I see a saving light
Rising from the sole remaining roots
Of the house of Oedipus. But this, too, falls
In a bloody harvest,   600
Claimed by the dust
Of the Underworld gods, doomed by foolish words
And frenzied wits.

[Strophe *b*]

O Zeus! Who could ever curtail thy power?
Not a man, never—   605
No matter how far he oversteps his bounds—
Not sleep, that weakens everyone,
Not the untiring months of gods.
No, Zeus, you do not grow weak with time,
You who hold power in the luminous glow of Olympus.   610
And this will be the law,
Now and for time to come, as it was before:
Madness stalks mortals who are great,
Leaves no escape from disaster.

[Antistrophe *b*]

Beware of hope! Far-reaching, beguiling, a pleasure—   615
For a lot of men.
But a lot are fooled by a light-headed love,
And deception stalks those who know nothing
Until they set their feet in fire and burn.
Wisdom lies in the famous proverb: 620
"Those who judge that crime is good,

601: See endnote.
605: "Man"—The Greek word *anêr* picks out the male of the species more often than not; to mean "human being" Greek uses *anthrôpos* or one of several words for "mortal." Because of the importance of gender issues in the play, I have observed the distinction throughout this translation.

Are in the hands of a driving god
Who is leading them to madness."
Time is very short for them,
625   Leaves no escape from disaster.

(Enter Haemon through the stage right wing.)

CHORUS:
Now, here is Haemon, the last of your children.
Is he goaded here by anguish for Antigone,
Who should have been his bride?
Does he feel injured beyond measure?
630   Cheated out of marriage?

CREON:
We'll know the answer right away, better than prophets:
Tell me, son, did you hear the final verdict?
Against your fiancée? Did you come in anger at your father?
Or are we still friends, no matter what I do?

HAEMON:
635   I am yours, Father. You set me straight,
Give me good advice, and I will follow it.
No marriage will weigh more with me,
Than your good opinion.

CREON:
Splendid, my boy! Keep that always in your heart,
640   And stand behind fatherly advice on all counts.
Why does a man pray that he'll conceive a child,
Keep him at home, and have him listen to what he's told?
It's so the boy will punish his father's enemies
And reward his friends—as his father would.
645   But some men beget utterly useless offspring:
They have planted nothing but trouble for themselves,
And they're nothing but a joke to their enemies.

624–5: See endnote.

626: Haemon would have been played either by the actor who represented Antigone or by the one who represented Ismene.

635: "I am yours"—your what? friend, child, enemy? Haemon is ambiguous here as elsewhere in this scene, careful not to criticize his father directly until he has been goaded out of decency.

Now then, my boy, don't let pleasure cloud your mind,
Not because of a woman. You know very well:
You'll have a frigid squeeze between the sheets   650
If you shack up with a hostile woman. I'd rather have
A bleeding wound than a criminal in the family.
So spit her out. And because the girl's against us,
Send her down to marry somebody in Hades.
You know I caught her in the sight of all,   655
Alone of all our people, in open revolt.
And I will make my word good in Thebes—
By killing her. Who cares if she sings "Zeus!"
And calls him her protector? I must keep my kin in line.
Otherwise, folks outside the family will run wild.   660
The public knows that a man is just
Only if he is straight with his relatives.

So, if someone goes too far and breaks the law,
Or tries to tell his masters what to do,
He will have nothing but contempt from me.   665
But when the city takes a leader, you must obey,
Whether his commands are trivial, or right, or wrong.
And I have no doubt that such a man will rule well,
And, later, he will cheerfully be ruled by someone else.
In hard times he will stand firm with his spear   670
Waiting for orders, a good, law-abiding soldier.

But reject one man ruling another, and that's the worst.
Anarchy tears up a city, divides a home,
Defeats an alliance of spears.
But when people stay in line and obey,   675
Their lives and everything else are safe.
For this reason, order must be maintained,
And there must be no surrender to a woman.
No! If we fall, better a man should take us down.
Never say that a woman bested us!   680

663–71: See endnote.

669: "And, later, he will cheerfully be ruled by someone else"—Creon
had been appointed regent when the sons of Oedipus were young, but
in the recent battle he served under Eteoclês. See endnote to lines 663–71
for an alternative meaning.

CHORUS:
   Unless old age has stolen my wits away,
   Your speech was very wise. That's my belief.

HAEMON:
   Father, the gods give good sense to every human being,
   And that is absolutely the best thing we have.
685 But if what you said is not correct,
   I have no idea how I could make the point.
   Still, maybe someone else could work it out.

   My natural duty's to look out for you, spot any risk
   That someone might find fault with what you say or do.
690 The common man, you see, lives in terror of your frown;
690a He'll never dare to speak up in broad daylight
   And say anything you would hate to learn.
   But I'm the one who hears what's said at night—
   How the entire city is grieving over this girl.
   No woman has ever had a fate that's so unfair
695 (They say), when what she did deserves honor and fame.
   She saved her very own brother after he died,
   Murderously, from being devoured by flesh-eating dogs
   And pecked apart by vultures as he lay unburied.
   For this, hasn't she earned glory bright as gold?
700 This sort of talk moves against you, quietly, at night.

   And for me, Father, your continued good fortune
   Is the best reward that I could ever have.
   No child could win a greater prize than his father's fame,
   No father could want more than abundant success—

---

683 ff.: Haemon's speech is carefully worded; he guards himself, by means of a series of ambiguities, from openly criticizing his father's judgment.

687: Although Haemon modestly implies that he is not capable of refuting his father, he also suggests that his father might be refutable. See endnote on this and on the next two lines for alternative readings.

690a: A line has apparently dropped out of the manuscripts; I have supplied this one to suit the context, against the advice of Lloyd-Jones and Wilson (LJW).

693: "The entire city is grieving"—If so, Antigone has not heard about it (see lines 847, 881–2). Haemon may be too far gone in love to be a credible witness, but his claim that common people are afraid to speak to Creon is corroborated by the Watchman's scenes.

From his son.

        And now, don't always cling to the same anger,   705
Don't keep saying that this, and nothing else, is right.
If a man believes that he alone has a sound mind,
And no one else can speak or think as well as he does,
Then, when people study him, they'll find an empty book.
But a wise man can learn a lot and never be ashamed;   710
He knows he does not have to be rigid and close-hauled.
You've seen trees tossed by a torrent in a flash flood:
If they bend, they're saved, and every twig survives,
But if they stiffen up, they're washed out from the roots.
It's the same in a boat: if a sailor keeps the footline taut,   715
If he doesn't give an inch, he'll capsize, and then—
He'll be sailing home with his benches down and his hull
   to the sky.
So ease off, relax, stop being angry, make a change.
I know I'm younger, but I may still have good ideas;
And *I* say that the oldest idea, and the best,   720
Is for one man to be born complete, knowing everything.
Otherwise—and it usually does turn out otherwise—
It's good to learn from anyone who speaks well.

CHORUS:
   Sir, you should learn from him, if he is on the mark. And you,
   Haemon, learn from your father. Both sides spoke well.   725

CREON: *(To the chorus.)*
   Do you really think, at our age,
   We should be taught by a boy like him?

HAEMON:
   No. Not if I am in the wrong. I admit I'm young;

715: A footline is the rope that runs from the foot of the sail, equivalent to what today's sailors call a sheet. Easing the sheet can save a boat from capsizing in a sudden gust of wind.

720–1: "The oldest idea" —The Greek word suggests precedence in rank in a way that would appeal to a conservative like Creon. Contrast this with Haemon's earlier and more democratic idea that every human being is endowed by nature with good sense (683), where "human beings" contrasts with "the man" at 721 and "good sense" (*phrenes*, intelligence) contrasts with "knowing everything." See endnote for an alternative reading.

That's why you should look at what I do, not my age.

CREON:

730   So "what you do" is show respect for breaking ranks?

HAEMON:

I'd never urge you to show respect for a criminal.

CREON:

So you don't think this girl has been infected with crime?

HAEMON:

No. The people of Thebes deny it, all of them.

CREON:

So you think the people should tell me what orders to give?

HAEMON:

735   Now who's talking like he's wet behind the ears?

CREON:

So I should rule this country for someone other than myself?

HAEMON:

A place for one man alone is not a city.

CREON:

A city belongs to its master. Isn't that the rule?

HAEMON:

Then go be ruler of a desert, all alone. You'd do it well.

CREON: *(To the chorus.)*

740   It turns out this boy is fighting for the woman's cause.

HAEMON:

Only if *you* are a woman. All I care about is you!

CREON:

This is intolerable! You are accusing your own father.

HAEMON:

Because I see you going wrong. Because justice matters!

CREON:

Is that wrong, showing respect for my job as leader?

744–5: Haemon holds that the respect Creon demands as leader cannot be separated from the wider virtue of reverence. By "the rights (or

HAEMON:
You have no respect at all if you trample on the rights of gods! 745

Creon:
What a sick mind you have: You submit to a woman!

Haemon:
No. You'll never catch me giving in to what's shameful.

Creon:
But everything you say, at least, is on her side.

Haemon:
And on your side! And mine! And the gods' below!

Creon:
There is no way you'll marry her, not while she's still alive. 750

Haemon:
Then she'll die, and her death will destroy Someone Else.

Creon:
Is that a threat? Are you brash enough to attack me?

Haemon:
What threat? All I'm saying is, you haven't thought this
through.

CREON:
I'll make you wish you'd never had a thought in your
empty head!

HAEMON:
If you weren't my father I'd say you were out of your mind. 755

CREON:
Don't beat around the bush. You're a woman's toy, a slave.

HAEMON:
Talk, talk, talk! Why don't you ever want to listen?

CREON:
Really? Listen, you are not going on like this. By all the gods,
One more insult from you, and the fun is over.

---

honors) of the gods," Haemon means that Creon wants to deprive Hades
of the dead man who belongs to them.
753: See endnote for an alternative reading.

(To attendants.)

760   Bring out that hated thing. I want her to die right here,
       Right now, so her bridegroom can watch the whole thing.

HAEMON:
       Not me. Never. No matter what you think.
       She is not going to die while I am near her.
       And you will never, ever see my face again. Go on,
765   Be crazy! Perhaps some of your friends will stay by you.

       (Exit Haemon through the stage left wing.)

CHORUS:
       Sir, the man has gone. He is swift to anger;
       Pain lies heavily on a youthful mind.

CREON:
       Let him go, him and his lofty ambitions! Good riddance!
       But those two girls shall not escape their fate.

CHORUS:
770   Are you really planning to kill *both* of them?

CREON:
       Not the one who never touched the crime. You're right.

CHORUS:
       By what means will you have the other one killed?

CREON:
       I'll take her off the beaten track, where no one's around,
       And I'll bury her alive underground, in a grave of stone.
775   I'll leave her only as much food as religious law prescribes,
       So that the city will not be cursed for homicide.

       Let her pray to Hades down there; he's the only god
       That she respects. Maybe she'll arrange for him to save her life;
       Maybe she'll learn, at last, that she's wasting her time
780   Showing respect for whatever's in Hades.

780: What does Creon do during the choral passage that follows? Probably he goes offstage so that he may give detailed orders for Antigone's
execution. Some editors, however, would have him remain backstage or
in the wings.

(Exit Creon through the great doors.)

Third Stasimon

CHORUS:

[Strophe]

In battle the victory goes to Love;
Prizes and properties fall to Love.
Love dallies the night
On a girl's soft cheeks,
Ranges across the sea,   785
Lodges in wild meadows.
O Love, no one can hide from you:
You take gods who live forever,
You take humans who die in a day,
And they take you and go mad.   790

[Antistrophe]

Destroyer Love, you seize a good mind,
And pervert it to wickedness:
This fight is your doing,
This uproar in the family.
And the winner will be desire,   795
Shining in the eyes of a bride,
An invitation to bed,
A power to sweep across the bounds of what is Right.
For we are only toys in your hands,
Divine, unbeatable Aphrodite!   800

Kommos

(Enter Antigone under guard through the great doors.)

CHORUS:
Now I, too, am swept away,
Out of bounds, when I see this.

798: See endnote for an alternative reading.

801: "I, too"—The chorus find themselves carried away by forbidden
feelings, as they say happened earlier to Haemon.

I cannot contain the surge of tears:
For now I see Antigone, soon to gain
805   The marriage bed where everyone must sleep.

ANTIGONE:
See how I walk the last road,
You who belong to my city,
How I fill my eyes with the last
Shining of the sun.
810   There's no return: I follow death, alive,
To the brink of Acheron,
Where He gives rest to all.
No marriage hymns for me.
No one sounds
815   A wedding march:
I will be the bride of Acheron.

CHORUS:
But won't you have hymns of praise?
So much glory attends you
As you pass into the deep place of the dead.
820   For you are not wasted by disease, not maimed by a
        sword.
But true to your own laws, you are the only one,
Of mortals, who'll go down to Hades while still alive.

ANTIGONE:
No. I hear Niobe was lost in utmost misery—
Daughter of Tantalus, visitor in Thebes,

816: Acheron—a river in the Underworld.

821: "But true to your own laws"—The Greek is *autonomos*, rendered by some scholars as "of your own will"; but the word means more than that in ancient Greek, and the root word "law" (*nomos*) is clearly heard. See Introduction, p. xviii on Antigone's law.

822: "While still alive"—The chorus mean that she will be entombed while still alive.

823–38: Niobe—Antigone misunderstands the chorus to be saying that she will live forever underground and cites the case of Niobe, who was entombed alive and then turned to stone. Niobe had many children and boasted of them by comparison with Leto, who had only two children, Artemis and Apollo. For this she was punished by seeing her children die of disease.

Wasted on a Phrygian mountain.   825
Rock sprouted up around her, firm,
Erect as shoots of ivy,
And it subdued her. So men say.
Rain and snow pelted her
Without a break, and she melted away,
Dripping from her mournful brows,   830
Tears streaming down her flanks.
It's the same for me, exactly:
Something divine lays me to sleep.

CHORUS:
Really! Niobe was a god; she had a god for a father.
We are mortal, and our fathers pass away.   835
But you—when you die, you will be great,
You will be equal in memory to the gods,
By the glory of your life and death.

ANTIGONE:
You're laughing at me.
For the gods' sake, why now?   840
You could have waited till I'm gone.
But now you make insults to my face,
You grasping, rich old men! What a city you have!
I call on the rising of rivers in Thebes
And on the great chariot-reaches of the plain.   845
The rivers and the plain are on my side, at least.
They'll testify that no friends wept for me,
That the laws of Thebes sent me to prison
In a rock-hollowed tomb.
They see how unusual and cruel this is.   850
But I have no place with human beings,
Living or dead. No city is home to me.

CHORUS:
You've gone too far! You are extreme, impetuous.
My child, you caught your foot and fell
When you tried to climb against high justice.   855
This is your father's legacy—pain and punishment.

ANTIGONE:
Now you raise the agony that hurts my mind the most:
Grief for my father,

Like raw earth plowed three times,
860 Grief for the whole huge disaster of *us*,
Our brilliant family,
Labdacus' descendants.
I weep for the ruin in my mother's bed,
The sexual intercourse and the incest
865 My father had with our mother.
Ill-fated parents make a miserable child.
I am going to them now,
Unholy and unmarried, to lodge with them.
Oh, my brother, you were married once,
870 But what a disaster it was:
Your death snuffed out my life.

CHORUS:
You have one kind of reverence.
But a man whose job it is to rule
Will never let you trample on his power.
875 You chose anger, and anger destroyed you.

ANTIGONE:
No tears for me, no friends, no wedding hymns.
They are taking me away
In misery by the road before me,
Now and forever forbidden to see
880 This blessed eye of light.
No friends cry for me,
No one is mourning.

(Enter Creon with his attendants through the
great doors.)

CREON:
Singing and wailing? They would never end
Before death, if they made any difference.
885 Take her away immediately. And when she's locked up,
In the embrace of her covered tomb—exactly as I said—
Leave her alone, deserted. Let her die if she wants,
Or else live there in her grave, if she feels at home there.

869: "You were married once"—Polyneices married the daughter of the
king of Argos, and Argos provided the army that attacked Thebes.

We wash our hands of this girl. But either way,
Her permit to reside above the earth is canceled.   890

ANTIGONE:
My tomb, my marriage, my hollow, scraped in dirt,
I'm coming home forever, to be held in
With my own people, most of them dead now,
And gone where Persephone welcomes them.
I am the last of them that will go under, and my death—   895
It is the worst by far—so much before my time.
As I leave, even so, I feed this one strong hope:
That I will have a loving welcome from my father,
More love from you, my mother, and then, love
From you, dear heart, my brother. When you died,   900
I took you up, all three, and laid you out,
And poured libations at your graves.
And, Polyneices, look: This is my reward
For taking care of you. I was right, but wisdom knows
I would not do it for a child, were I a mother,   905
Not for a husband either. Let them lie, putrefied, dead;
I would not defy the city at such cost for their sake.

What law can I claim on my side for this choice?
I may have another husband if the first should die
And get another child from a new man if I'm a widow.   910
But my mother and my father lie in the land of death,
And there is no ground to grow a brother for me now.
That is the law I followed when I made you first in honor,
Even though Creon thought I did a terrible thing,
A rash and sinful crime, dear heart, my brother.   915
Now he has taken me by force, he is driving me down
Unmarried. I've had no man, no wedding celebration,
Shared nothing with a husband, never raised a child.
My friends and family have abandoned me in misery,
And I am going—alive—to the scraped hollow of the dead.   920
What have I ever done against divine justice?
How can I expect a god to help me in my misery?
To whom should I pray now? Do you see?
They are counting all my reverence to be

904–20: See endnote.

925   Irreverence. If the gods really agree with this,
       Then suffering should teach me to repent my sin.
       But if the sin belongs to those who condemned me,
       I hope they suffer every bit as I do now.

CHORUS:
       Still she is tossed by gusts of wind;
930   They tear through her soul as strongly as before.

CREON:
       Listen, it's the guards who will weep
       If they don't get a move on now.

ANTIGONE (or CHORUS): *(With a cry of pain.)*
       That word—
       It's almost death itself!

CREON:
935   I have no hope to give.
       The death sentence stands.

ANTIGONE:
       City of my fathers, Thebes!
       Gods of my people!
       They are taking me against my will.
940   Look at me, O you lords of Thebes:
       I am the last remnant of kings.
       Look what these wretched men are doing to me,
       For my pure reverence!

Fourth Stasimon

CHORUS: *(To Antigone.)*

[Strophe *a*]

       Courage! Danaë, too, endured
945   The exchange of heavenly light
       For a bronze-bolted prison.
       And there she was kept down

944–50: Danaë's father locked her away from men because of an oracle warning him against any son she might bear. But Zeus visited her in a shower of gold, and they conceived a child, Perseus.

947: "Kept down"—yoke motif, cf. line 955.

Secretly in a bedroom tomb.
She was of noble birth, too, my daughter, O my daughter,
And Zeus trusted her to mind his golden-rainfall child.   950
    Fate has a terrible power
    That nothing escapes, not wealth,
    Not warfare, not a fortress tower,
    Not even black ships beating against the sea.

[Antistrophe *a*]

Another case: Lycurgus was kept down,   955
And he was a king in Thrace.
But because of his angry jeering,
Dionysus had him jailed in a cell of rock,
And there the terrible flood-force
Of his madness trickled away, drop by drop, until he learned,   960
At last, that it was a god he had stung in his madness
    With those jeering insults.
    For he tried to quench the holy fire,
    Reined in the god-filled women,
    And drove flute-loving Muses into a rage.   965

[Strophe *b*]

At the Black Waters,
Where a thrust of land divides the Bosporus from the Sea,

955–65: Lycurgus had tried to suppress the worship of Dionysus, which involved ecstatic rituals. In some versions of the story, he went mad and killed his son before being imprisoned.

958: Dionysus was believed by the ancient Greeks to have brought his worship to Greece from Asia, along with the practice of making wine. See Euripides' play, the *Bacchae*.

964: "God-filled women"—These women, variously called Maenads, Bacchae, and bacchants, are women who worship Dionysus through ecstatic dance and song in the mountains, away from their homes. "God-filled" means "inspired."

965: "Flute-loving Muses": The *aulos*, usually translated "flute," was a reed instrument; its music was considered to be the most exciting in ancient Greece.

966–87: Phineus, a king in Thrace (northern Greece), had two sons by

Lies a city of Thrace known as Salmydéssus.
War god Ares was hard by and saw the curséd blows
970   When Phineus' two sons were blinded by the beast
          He called a wife. Darkness came
          Over the disks that had been eyes,
          That would have looked for vengeance
          To gashing hands, stained in blood,
975   Shuttles torn from the loom
          And used as knives.

[Antistrophe *b*]

The boys melted away
In misery, mourning their own sad fate
And their mother's, for her marriage was hateful
980   Although she was born to be a queen of the ancient line,
Royal in Athens, and she was raised in distant caves
          Where her father's tempests blew.
          For he was North Wind, Boreas,
          And she was a child of gods,
985   Swift as horses on a rocky slope.
          But the eternal Fates kept after her,
          Her too, O my daughter.

*(As the chorus bring their ode to an end, the
attendants lead Antigone out through the stage left
wing. Enter Tiresias, led by a boy, through the stage
right wing.)*

his first wife, Cleopatra (no relation to the famous queen of Egypt). This
Cleopatra was the daughter of an Athenian princess who had been stolen
by Boreas, the North Wind, to be his bride. Cleopatra's sons were blinded
by their stepmother after Phineus had imprisoned their mother and
taken a new wife. The audience, probably knowing about the impris-
onment of the mother, would have seen the analogy with the fate of
Antigone.

966: "Black Waters"—The manuscripts are unclear. The phrase may
refer to the Black Sea or the two Dark Islands at the mouth of the
Bosporus.

973: "Vengeance"—Had the boys not been blinded, they would have
avenged the crime against their mother.

980: "Born to be a queen"—Here we follow the text as corrected by LJW.

TIRESIAS: *(To the chorus, indicating the boy who guides him.)*
  Gentlemen of Thebes, we two have come by the same path;
  He alone has eyesight, and we both see by this:
  A blind man takes the way his guide directs.   990

CREON:
  Why, old Tiresias! What brings you here?

TIRESIAS:
  I will speak: I am the soothsayer, and you will learn.

CREON:
  Well, I never have rejected your advice.

TIRESIAS:
  That is how you've been steering the city straight.

CREON:
  Yes, I know firsthand how helpful you are, and I can testify.   995

TIRESIAS:
  Then know this: Once again, your fate stands on a
    knife-edge.

CREON:
  What is it? Your voice puts my hair on end!

TIRESIAS:
                                              You'll see.
  Listen to what I have read from the signs of my art.
  I took my seat, the ancient seat for seeing omens—
  Where all the birds that tell the future come to rest—   1000
  And I heard a voice I've never known from a bird:
  Wild screeching, enraged, utterly meaningless.
  But the thrashing of their wings told me the truth:
  They were clawing each other to death with their talons.
  I was frightened. Immediately, I tried burnt sacrifice.   1005

988: Tiresias announces his own arrival. Unlike the previous entrances, this one is unexpected by both Creon and the chorus. During the fourth stasimon, Creon has evidently remained on stage, but without paying close attention to the chorus.

999: "I took my seat"—Tiresias read the omens of the birds from a seat in a sacred spot.

1005: "Burnt sacrifice"—Ancient Greeks offered thighbones wrapped in

The altar had been blazing high, but not one spark
Caught fire in my offerings. The embers went out.
Juice was oozing and dripping from thighbones,
Spitting and sputtering in clouds of smoke.
1010 Bladders were bursting open, spraying bile into the sky;
Wrappings of fat fell away from soggy bones.

And so the ritual failed; I had no omens to read.
I learned this from the boy who is my guide,
As I am the guide for others. Now, it was *your* idea
1015 That brought this plague down on our city.
Every single altar, every hearth we have,
Is glutted with dead meat from Oedipus' child,
Who died so badly. Birds and dogs gnawed him to bits
That is why the gods no longer hear our prayers,
1020 Reject our sacrifice of flaming thighbones. And that is why
The birds keep back their shrill message-bearing cries:
Because they have fed on a dead man's glistening blood.

Take thought, my son, on all these things:
It's common knowledge, any human being can go wrong.
1025 But even when he does, a man may still succeed:
He may have his share of luck and good advice
But only if he's willing to bend and find a cure
For the trouble he's caused. It's only being stubborn
Proves you're a fool.

So, now, surrender to the dead man.
1030 Stop stabbing away at his corpse. Will it prove your strength
If you kill him again? Listen, my advice is for your benefit.
Learning from good words is sweet when they bring you
gain.

CREON:
I hear you, old man: You people keep shooting arrows at me
Like marksmen at a target. Do you think I don't know?
1035 I have a lot of experience with soothsayers. Your whole tribe

fat to the gods, along with other inedible parts of a cow or sheep, by burning these parts on an altar.
1019–23: See lines 1042–4, with note.

Has made market of me from the start. "Benefit"? "Gain"?
If you want to turn a profit, speculate in gold from India
Or go trade with Sardis for electrum and traffic in that.
You'll never put that man down in a grave,
Not even if eagles snatched morsels of his dead flesh   1040
And carried them up to the very throne of Zeus.
I won't shrink from that. And don't you call it "pollution"
Or tell me I have to bury him to fend off miasma—
Surely no human power could pollute a god.

You're terribly clever, old man, but listen to me: 1045
Clever people tend to stumble into shameful traps
When they make a wicked speech sound good
For their personal gain.

TIRESIAS:
                          This is very sad:
Does any human being know, or even question . . .

CREON: *(Interrupting.)*
What's this? More of your great "common knowledge"?

TIRESIAS:
How powerful good judgment is, compared to wealth.   1050

CREON:
Exactly. And no harm compares with heedlessness.

TIRESIAS:
Which runs through you like the plague.

CREON:
I have no desire to trade insults with a soothsayer.

TIRESIAS:
But you're doing it. You implied that I make false prophecies.

1038: Electrum is an alloy of gold and silver made in Sardis, the city
where Croesus, famous for his wealth, had ruled in the sixth century.

1042–4: Pollution, miasma—Either an unburied corpse or an unavenged
murder was thought to infect the land with *miasma*, pollution. Creon dis-
misses this on rational grounds.

1045: "Terribly clever"—The Greek word *deinos* carries both positive and
negative meanings. See line 332, with note.

CREON:

1055 Prophecies? All your tribe wants to make is money.

TIRESIAS:

And what about tyrants? Filthy lucre is all you want!

CREON:

Remember, you are speaking about your commander-in-chief.

TIRESIAS:

I haven't forgotten. It was by my powers that you saved
 the city.

CREON:

Cunning soothsayer! Yes, but you'd rather do what's wrong.

TIRESIAS:

1060 You are provoking me. I have a secret we have not touched.

CREON:

Well, touch it then. But do not speak as you've been paid
 to do.

TIRESIAS:

Do you really think that's why I've spoken out?

CREON:

You'll never collect your fee; I'm not changing *my* mind.

TIRESIAS:

So be it. But you must know this and know it well:
1065 You'll hardly see the sun race around its course
Before you'll make a trade with your own boy's corpse—
Your only child, born from your guts, traded for corpses.

You took one who dwells above and tossed her below,
You rejected a living soul and peopled a tomb with her.
1070 And you took one who belongs down there and kept him
 here,
Untouched by gods, unburied, unholy, a corpse exposed.
The dead are no business of yours; not even the gods above
Own any part of them. You've committed violence against
 them.

1067: See line 626. Haemon is Creon's last surviving child.

For this, an ambush awaits you—slow, crippling avengers,
Furies sent by Hades and the gods above.   1075
You will be tangled in the net of your own crimes.

Now look carefully: Have I been paid to speak out?
No. The passage of a little time will prove the point;
Men and women will be wailing over death in your family.
And all the cities of our enemies are in a rage   1080
For their dead, whose funeral rites were held by dogs
Or wild beasts or vultures, and for the stench of bodies
Carried by birds to defile their hearths at home.

These are my arrows. You stung me, and I let fly,
In my anger, like a marksman aiming for your heart.   1085
And I never miss. You can't outrun the pain.

    (To his guide.)

Take us home, boy.
Let him vent his anger on younger men;
May he learn to cultivate a gentler tongue
And a mind more cogent than he has shown today.   1090

    *(Exit Tiresias led by the boy through the stage right
    wing.)*

CHORUS:
    The man is gone, sir. His prophecies were amazing,
    Terrible. Ever since my hair turned white
    I'm quite certain he has never sung a prophecy,
    Not once, that turned out to be false for the city.

CREON:
    I know that, too. My mind is shaken.   1095
    Giving in would be terrible.
    But standing firm invites disaster!

1075: Furies—avenging spirits.

1080–3: These lines refer to the tradition, not otherwise mentioned in this
play, that Creon left not just Polyneices but all the enemy troops unburied.
See Introduction, p. ix. (Some editors reject these lines as spurious in order
to maintain the consistency of the play.)

1091–2: "His prophecies were amazing, terrible"—same double-edged
word (*deinos*) as in line 1045, here translated "amazing, terrible."

CHORUS:
Good judgment is essential, Creon. Take advice.

CREON:
What should I do? Show me. I'll do what you say.

CHORUS:
1100   Let the girl go. Free her from underground.
And build a tomb for the boy who lies exposed.

CREON:
Really? You think I should give in?

CHORUS:
As quickly as you can, sir, before you're cut off.
The gods send Harm racing after wicked fools.

CREON:
1105   It's so painful to pull back; it goes against my heart.
But I cannot fight against necessity.

CHORUS:
Go and do this *now*. Don't send others in your place.

CREON:
I'll go immediately. Come on, come on, everyone,
Wherever you are, grab a pick and shovel,
1110   Hurry up! Get over to the place you see.
It's up to me, now my mind has changed.
I put her away, I must be there to release her.
I'm afraid it is best to obey the laws,
Just as tradition has them, all one's life.

(*Exit Creon, with his attendants, through the stage
left wing.*)

CHORUS:

Fifth Stasimon

[Strophe *a*]

1115   God of many names,

1115: "God of many names"—Dionysus is known by a number of names, including the ones the chorus use here, "Bacchus" and "Iacchus."

Glorious child of Thebes,
Whose mother was bride
To Zeus' deep thunder!
It is you who guard the fame of Italy,
You who look after the embrace, at Eleusis,   1120
Of Demeter, all-welcoming goddess.
O Bacchus, your home is Thebes,
Thebes, the mother of Maenads,
Where River Ismenus gently flows,
And the fierce dragon-teeth were planted.   1125

[Antistrophe *a*]

Torches flash through smoke,
Catch sight of you at Delphi
High above the twin-peaked crag.
The Castalian Stream has seen you
By nymphs of the cave who dance for Bacchus.   1130
The Nysaean Mountains know you, too,
The ivy-covered shores, the coasts,
The green tangles of grapevines.
They are sending you to Thebes: Watch over us,
Hear our sacred hymns that sound for you.   1135

1117: The line refers to the mother of Bacchus. Semélê was a princess of
Thebes who became pregnant with Dionysus, after being visited by Zeus,
and gave birth to the infant god when Zeus struck her with thunder.

1119: Italy—Dionysus was evidently honored in the Greek cities of south-
ern Italy.

1123: "Maenads"—See the note on line 964.

1124–5: The Ismenus flows through Thebes. According to legend, Cadmus founded Thebes by killing a dragon and planting its teeth as seeds;
where he planted them, the warriors of Thebes sprouted from the earth.

1127: Delphi—Though sacred mainly to Apollo, Delphi was also a prin-
cipal site for the worship of Dionysus.

1129: The Castalian Stream flows from a sacred spring at Delphi.

1130: Nymphs were minor divinities believed to inhabit caves and other
special places.

1131: Nysaean Mountains—probably refers to mountains on the long
island of Euboea, separated from Attica by a narrow strait.

[Strophe *b*]

You hold Thebes in honor
Above all cities;
Your mother, too,
Thunderstruck woman.
1140   And now we pray: Watch over us:
The violence of plague
Strikes all our people.
Come, your presence is healing.
Soar above Parnassus
1145   Or cross the howling straits of the sea.

[Antistrophe *b*]

O Leader in the dance of stars,
That circle across the night,
Breathing fire,
O shepherd of dark voices,
1150   Child of Zeus, let us see you now.
Come, O Lord, with your throng of Maenads
Iacchus, steward of joy,
Grant them ecstasy
To dance all night for you.

(Enter Messenger through the stage left wing.)

MESSENGER:
1155   Listen, all you neighbors of Cadmus' family:
The course of our lives never stops; it runs past good
Or ill. I'll never declare success or failure for anyone.
It's only chance that keeps your boat upright,
And chance that sinks you—good luck or bad is all you have.
1160   Soothsayers give no guarantees for human lives.
This Creon—you know, I used to envy him.
He saved the land of Cadmus from its enemies
And took command as the only ruler of this ground.

1143: "Come, your presence is healing"—A more literal version would
be "Come on cleansing foot." The chorus means that Dionysus' presence
would purify Thebes and so save its people from the plague.

1144: Parnassus is the high mountain dividing Thebes from Delphi.

He set us straight, and he set his house abloom
With well-born sons. Now all of that is gone.   1165
When every source of joy deserts a man,
I don't call him alive: he's an animated corpse.
For my money, you can get as rich as you want,
You can wear the face of a tyrant,
But if you have no joy in this,   1170
Your life's not worth the shadow of a puff of smoke.

CHORUS:
What's this new grief that weighs on the king's family?

MESSENGER:
Death. And the living are to blame for it.

CHORUS:
Who's the killer? Who's the victim? Speak up!

MESSENGER:
Haemon is dead, killed by his own flesh and blood.   1175

CHORUS:
What! His father? Some other relative?

MESSENGER:
He killed himself, in a rage with his father, for her death.

CHORUS:
That soothsayer! He had it right.

MESSENGER:
Those are the facts; the judgment is up to you.

(Enter Eurydice through the great doors.)

CHORUS:
Wait, I see her coming, Creon's wife.   1180
Poor Eurydice, has she heard about her son?
Or did she leave her home by chance?

EURYDICE:
Tell me, men of the city—I caught what you said
As I was about to leave the house
To pray for help to the goddess Athena.   1185
I was just sliding the bolt to unlock the door
When word of disaster in the family struck my ears.

I fell back into my servants' arms,
Terrified out of my mind.

1190   Please tell me again. What happened?
Speak freely. I am quite used to hearing bad news.

MESSENGER:
I will, beloved queen. I was *there*,
And I'll tell you everything, the whole truth.
No point taking off the rough edges;

1195   You'd soon find out I was lying. Truth's right,
Always.
            Well, I went with your husband as his guide
To the upper field where the body was lying,
What was left of Polyneices—Cruel!—torn by dogs.
First we prayed to the goddess of passageways,

1200   Pluto also, and we begged that their good will attend us.
Then we performed the sacred cleansing of the corpse,
Gathered up the pieces we could find,
Burned them over fresh-cut boughs,
And heaped up the earth into a tomb,
A high-crested home for him.

1205   Then we went for the girl,
Toward her deadly marriage bed, blanketed with rocks.
There was a voice—you could hear it from far off—
It sliced through you, wailing around that unsanctified
    tomb.
One of us got Creon to listen. He crept forward; cries of
    misery

1210   Welled up around him, wordless, without meaning.
Suddenly he let out a groan of utter despair—
"Oh no! Now *I* am reading signs: Could this be the path?
The one that that leads me to the worst disaster of my life?
My son! My son's voice! Neighbors, be quick, please help.

1215   On the tomb, look, that gap in the mound—
Stones ripped out—can you slip in through those jaws?

1199–1200: Hecate, goddess of passageways (including the one to the
Underworld), was honored along roads, especially at intersections. Pluto,
also called Hades, is god of the Underworld.

1212: "Now *I* am reading signs"—Creon has taken on the role of Tiresias by finding meanings in inarticulate cries.

Tell me if I am right, that it *is* Haemon,
Unless the gods have robbed me of my mind."

That was the order our master gave, his courage gone.
We looked. In the last depth of the tomb,   1220
She was there, we saw her hanging by the neck
On a noose she'd twisted from her own fine clothes.
He was there, too, tumbled around her, hugging her waist,
Grieving for his marriage lost, gone under—
His father's doing—as he, in misery, kissed his bride.   1225
When Creon saw them, he gave a horrible cry
And came up to them. He was in tears, sobbing:
"Poor soul," he said, "how could you do this?
What were you thinking? Had you lost your mind?
O my child, come out, please, I beg you on my knees."   1230
The boy did not answer. His eyes were fierce.
He fixed them on his father, then spat in his face
And drew his two-edged sword. The father darted back,
Dodged the blow. Thwarted, the angry boy
Turned against himself. He took his blade   1235
And leaned on it, drove it half through his lungs.
Then, still conscious, he pulled the girl into the curve
Of his sagging embrace. He gasped and panted,
Spattered blood on her white cheek, a spurt of scarlet.
Then he was dead. His body lay with hers;   1240
They'd brought their marriage off at last in the house
    of Death—
Which proves the point: In a human life,
It's deadly for bad judgment to embrace a man.

   (Exit Eurydice through the great doors.)

CHORUS:
   What could it mean? The woman's gone inside.
   She did not stay for a word, good or bad.   1245

1227: "And came up to them"—The manuscripts read "came up to him."
Some editors prefer "came up to her" so that Creon's first two lines can
be understood as spoken to Antigone's corpse. But Creon may well be
using those lines to address Haemon for his desperate breaking into the
tomb. I have chosen "them" in order to preserve the ambiguity. Let the
reader choose.

MESSENGER:
I'm astonished, like you. But I feed on hope. Probably,
When she heard her son was dead, she chose to mourn
  indoors,
Rather than make a public display of grief.
She'll have her servants join in the lament.
1250   She's always planned ahead, to avoid mistakes.

CHORUS:
I don't know. If you ask me, a silence so extreme
Is as dangerous as a flood of silly tears.

MESSENGER:
We'll know soon enough if she's holding something in,
And hiding it secretly in a seething heart.
1255   I'm going into the house. You may be right:
Silence, when extreme, is dangerous.

(*Exit Messenger through the great doors. Creon
enters through the stage left wing; assisted by his
attendants, he is carrying the body of Haemon.*)

CHORUS:
Now here is the king himself. He carries in his arms
A Reminder (I hope I'm right to be blunt)
Pointing clearly to the madness that destroys,
1260   And it's no one else's but his own. The sin was his.

[Strophe *a*]

CREON:
Oh, howl for the sins of a stubborn mind,
Evil-minded, death-dealing! O you who are witnesses,
You saw those who killed and those who died,
All in one family,
1265   Cry out against the sacrilege that I called strategy!
Oh, howl, my son, my young son, for your young death.
Ah! Ah!
You were expelled from life
By my bad judgment, never yours.

1259: "Madness that destroys"—*atê.* See note on lines 584–5.

CHORUS:
Yes, it is late, but you have seen where justice lies.   1270

[Strophe *b*]

CREON:
Oh yes:
I have learned, and it is misery.
Some god leapt full force onto my head
And steered me onto a wild path, shaking my reins,
And I have trampled joy with sharp hooves.   1275
Oh weep, weep for the pain of human pain!

(*Enter Messenger through the great doors.*)

MESSENGER:
You have so many troubles, master, troubles in hand—
You carry them yourself. And troubles at home—
You'll see them for yourself, soon enough, when you arrive.   1280

CREON:
What, after this, could be worse?

MESSENGER:
Your wife is dead, poor woman.
Fresh-killed, a mother to match this dead boy.

[Antistrophe *a*]

CREON:
Howl, howl! O Death, refuge that cannot be appeased,
Why me? Why me, Destroyer?

(*To the Messenger.*)

                                        And you,   1285
What is this noise you're making? Your horrible message?
It is only grief.
I was a man in ruins, and you crushed me again.
Speak to me, my son, tell me, is there more killing?
Ah! Ah!   1290
Is it a woman's sacrifice,
Her death piled on yours?

(The great doors open, and Eurydice's body is brought out or revealed.)

CHORUS (or MESSENGER):
Look, she is here, brought out from the inner rooms.

[Antistrophe *b*]

CREON:
Oh yes:
1295 Here's the second disaster for my misery to see.
What could be worse? Does fate have more for me?
A moment ago, I took my dead son in my arms.
Now I see her face to face—my wife. And she is dead.
Oh weep, weep for the mother in torment, weep for the child.

MESSENGER:
1300 She died at the altar.
A sharp sword-thrust brought darkness to her eyes,
But first she grieved over Megareus, dead before his
        wedding,
And then over Haemon.
Last of all she called out to you,
1305 "These are your crimes, Childkiller!"

[Strophe *c*]

CREON:
Ah! Ah!
I am on wings of fear.
Take a sharp sword, someone.
Why don't you kill me now?
1310 My misery is so huge,
I am dissolved in misery.

MESSENGER:
Yes, she brought this charge against you as she died:
"You're to blame for his death, and the other boy's, too."

1302: Megareus—Haemon's only brother, son of Creon and Eurydice. The audience probably knew that Megareus had been sacrificed earlier to ensure victory over Argos.

CREON:
　　Tell me, how was she killed?

MESSENGER:
　　Stabbed in the guts by her own hand,　　　　　　　　　1315
　　As soon as she heard what horrors came over her boy.

[Strophe *d*]

CREON:
　　The grief is mine, all mine.
　　I'll never pin the blame on anyone else that's human.
　　I was the one, I killed you, poor child.
　　I did it. It is all true.　　　　　　　　　　　　　　1320
　　Now, my neighbors,
　　Please take me away,
　　Take me quickly.
　　I must not be underfoot;
　　I am worth less than a nobody.　　　　　　　　　　　1325

CHORUS:
　　A worthy request—if there's any value in suffering.
　　Shortest way is strongest way when trouble's afoot.

[Antistrophe *c*]

CREON:
　　Let it come! Let it come!
　　I look for the light
　　Of my last day.　　　　　　　　　　　　　　　　1330
　　My ultimate fate
　　Oh, let it come
　　I never want to face another day!

CHORUS:
　　That lies in the future. Our duty is for the present.
　　Leave your death to the Ones whose concern it is.　　　1335

CREON:
　　But that's what I long for. I prayed for that.

CHORUS:
　　Then don't pray at all.

A mortal has no escape from fate.

[Antistrophe *d*]

CREON: *(Praying.)*
　　　　Please take this useless man,
1340　　Put him out of your way. He killed you, my child,
　　　　Though that is not what he wished.
　　　　And you, too, my wife.

　　　　What a miserable wretch I am!
　　　　Never to see them again!
1345　　On whom can I lean?
　　　　Everything I touch turns against me,
　　　　My head bows to the fate that has leapt on it.

CHORUS:
　　　　Wisdom is supreme for a blesséd life,
　　　　And reverence for the gods
1350　　Must never cease.
　　　　Great words, sprung from arrogance,
　　　　Are punished by great blows.
　　　　So it is one learns, in old age, to be wise.

–END–

1348: "Wisdom is supreme for a blesséd life"—*Phronein* (wisdom, good sense) is essential for *eudaimonia* (flourishing, happiness in a broad sense).

Endnotes

Recent editors differ widely on how to read certain lines in *Antigone*. The new Oxford Classical Text of Lloyd-Jones and Wilson, supported by their *Sophoclea*, is fairly free with emendation. Griffith's Cambridge edition is more conservative, and so is the excellent new translation by Blundell. On the whole I have followed a conservative policy, translating the manuscript readings wherever possible. In the following notes I comment on passages for which different readings give significantly different results. LJW stands for Lloyd-Jones and Wilson.

Line 10: The Greek text allows three fairly literal translations: (1) "Evils from our enemies are advancing against our friends" (Lloyd-Jones and Griffith, whom I follow): (2) "Evils that are appropriate to our enemies are advancing against our friends" (Blundell); (3) "Evils inflicted on our enemies [i.e., the dead Argives] are advancing against our friends." In the first reading, Antigone takes Creon to be her enemy. In the second, she presupposes the principle that it is right to cause harm (such as non-burial) to one's enemies (on which see Blundell 1989). That principle has a place in ancient Greek tradition, but it has already been challenged by poets (including Homer) and does not appear to be supported elsewhere in this play. The general wisdom seems to be that Achilles goes too far in punishing Hector's corpse, and that Creon will err in the same way with the remains of Polyneices. The third reading refers to the punishment already inflicted on the Argive corpses according to the story that none of the Argives were granted burial—a story that Antigone does not elsewhere seem to know.

Line 97: LJW emends to read, "I shall suffer nothing so dire that my death will not be one of honor."

Line 157: The text is faulty here; the word "ruler" is a conjecture, and the word translated "new" is thought by some editors to be a mistake by a copyist. It is unparalleled in this usage.

Lines 167–8: LJW suspects a gap in the text in which we should supply a line such as "With my sister as his wife, you always served them faithfully." This provides an antecedent for "their" in "their sons" (line 168).

Line 369: "If he honors the law." Along with most editors, I translate an emended text. LJW and Blundell follow the manuscript reading "If he inserts the law . . . ," probably meaning "If he weaves the law into the fabric of his life, or of the city."

Lines 582–625: Second Stasimon. Although the general ideas are clear, the manuscripts are not; and editors have proposed a number of changes. I have kept as close as possible to the manuscript readings, while trying to convey a clear meaning to the audience or reader.

Line 601: "Claimed by the dust." Some editors emend the text to read "It is harvested by a bloody chopper."

Line 607: "Sleep, that weakens everyone"—so in the manuscripts. Most editors reject the manuscript reading, which more literally means "sleep, the all-aging one," because sleep does not by itself cause anyone to age. But the word for old age also connotes infirmity, and any sleeper is more feeble for being asleep.

Line 608: "The untiring months of gods"—so in the manuscripts. Most editors, including LJW, correct "gods" to "years." But the meaning in the manuscripts is fine: For gods, the procession of months goes on forever. "Untiring"—The procession of months never weakens for the gods, nor does it weaken them.

Line 613: "Madness stalks mortals who are great." The text given by the manuscripts is unreadable, but this cliché is the most likely.

Lines 624–5: "Time is very short for them / Leaves no time for disaster." LJW emends the text to read "The small man fares throughout his time without disaster."

Lines 663–71: I have followed the manuscripts, as has LJW; in 669 I translate *de* as "later," to bring out the alternations of power that it implies. Some editors, however, including Griffith, believe that lines 663–7 were transposed by copyists from their original place after 671. Then it is not the appointed leader who is willingly ruled by someone else, but the good citizen who plays his assigned role as leader in some contexts and as follower in others:

The public knows that a man is just	661
Only if he is straight with his relatives.	662
And I have no doubt that such a man will lead well	668
And will cheerfully be led by someone else.	669
In hard times he will stand firm with his spear	670
Waiting for orders, a good, law-abiding soldier.	671
So, if someone goes too far and breaks the law,	663
Or tries to tell his masters what to do,	664
He will have nothing but contempt from me.	665
But when the city takes a leader, you must obey,	666
Whether his commands are trivial, or right, or wrong.	667
But reject one man ruling another, and that's the worst.	672
Anarchy tears up a city, divides a home,	673
Defeats an alliance of spears.	674

Lines 666–7: Some editors find it hard to believe that Creon would demand obedience to orders that are wrong, and so they argue that these lines are not authentic.

Line 687: "Someone else." Some editors emend the line to give the meaning "Still, this [i.e., the job of refuting Creon] could be done in another way"; others, such as LJW, take it to mean "Still, another view might be correct." Some editors consider the line to be inauthentic.

Lines 688–9: "My natural duty"—so the majority of editors, including Blundell and Griffith. LJW read a variant, "But it is not in your nature to foresee people's words or actions. . . ." But it is not Creon's nature but his job that keeps him from hearing what people say about him (Griffith); Haemon can serve as his ears.

Lines 720–1: "And I say that the oldest idea. . . ." I am taking "every" (*panta*) as accusative of respect with "knowledge," rather than as modifying "man," which would give us "And *I* say that the oldest idea, and the best, / Is for every man to be born full of knowledge."

Line 753: "You haven't thought this through." LJW emends the text to yield the meaning "What kind of threat is it to tell you my decisions?" But a decision could well be a threat, and the word LJW would give up ("empty" in "your plans or thoughts are empty") is nicely picked up by the next line, as often in dialogue.

Line 798: Sexual love is "a power to sweep across the bounds of what is Right." I translate an emendation proposed by Griffith, which prepares the way for line 801. The reading of the manuscripts presents metrical difficulties as well as an implausible meaning: that desire is enthroned beside what is Right. "Right" translates "great *thesmoi*," which refers to a concept that is older and more fundamental than law or justice. No tradition gives Aphrodite such a throne; what she stands for is subversive of order.

Line 845: "Chariot-reaches of the plain." Some scholars take *alsos* to mean "grove," but "plain" is more likely in this context (Griffith). Chariots need open space.

Lines 904–20: Some editors reject these lines as spurious because they do not see how they can be consistent with Antigone's position that unwritten law requires all the dead to be buried. Virtually all recent editors accept the lines, however, and Foley (1996) has shown how suitable they are for Antigone. Note that Aristotle cites lines 911–2, alluding to the main argument of the passage, at *Rhetoric* 3.16, 1417a32–33.

Line 980: "Born to be a queen." Here I follow the text as emended by LJW.

Appendix: Hegel on *Antigone*

Hegel presents so many difficulties to the reader that "he is cited much more frequently than he is read and discussed far oftener than he is understood" (Wood 1991, p. xxvii). Although Hegel's influence on subsequent readings of *Antigone* has been powerful, many readers (such as Bradley 1950) overlook the importance of *Antigone* to Hegel's phenomenology. As a result, they miss the subtlety of Hegel's account of the play. Hegel's theory does not lend itself to summary, but here is a sketch of the main points that bear on *Antigone*.

Reading *Antigone* is not merely an aesthetic exercise for Hegel. Its heroine provides him a clear statement of the absoluteness of right. The unwritten laws Antigone cites simply *are*; they are beyond human investigation and evaluation: "If they are supposed to be validated by my insight, then I have already denied their unshakeable, intrinsic being . . ." (Miller 1977, 437, references by paragraph number).

Nature has assigned different ethical concerns to women than to men. Women guard the divine law on which family bonds depend; men guard the human law that supports community and government. But men grow up within the family, and women reside in the larger community, so the assignment by gender does not free either group to follow its own law without attention to the other. In any event, both laws are believed to be supported by gods, and, in Hegelian terms, both laws belong to the same ethical substance. But it is only by action—the kind of action taken in a tragic play—that a superior ethical consciousness comes, through suffering, to recognize this.

Because of her conscious action, Antigone is Hegel's clearest instance of ethical consciousness. "Ethical consciousness must recognize its opposite as its own actuality . . . it must recognize its guilt" (Shannon 2001, p. 24; Miller, 469). Antigone, Hegel says, commits her crime knowingly—or, more accurately, her knowledge comes with her action. In the case of Oedipus, Hegel says, "A power that shuns the daylight lies in wait for the ethical self-consciousness, and sallies out and catches it red-handed when the deed is done . . ." (Shannon, p. 24; Miller, 469). The power that ambushes a tragic character is the ethical power that he or she has been unable to recognize before committing the deed that brings it out into the open, represented by the god who is neglected by that character. Like her father, Antigone has been ambushed.

"Because we suffer, we recognize that we have erred," she says, according to Hegel, who is following Hölderlin's version of lines 925–6: "If this truly has now come before the gods, then we suffer and ask to be forgiven our past sins" (quoted in Shannon, p. 24 n41). Hegel must suppose that Antigone infers her error from her suffering, and that she understands this as an error of her entire community.

Antigone's admission of guilt—not just for herself, but for her community—is crucial to Hegel's appreciation of her. She is "the prophet of her epoch." Her recognition of error is "a death sentence on both herself and her community" (Shannon, p. 172). In her admission there is a kind of reconciliation of the two laws, because both are recognized. But the conflict remains, and it remains destructive to Antigone and her people. There remains no hope of redemption while the conflict is understood only as a contest between divine and human law. The ancient world and its fundamental conflict must be superseded by the modern world and its conflict between faith and reason. This supersession, however does not leave Spirit, the subject that realizes itself in history, untouched by tension between the two laws; that tension continues to animate the movement by which Spirit comes to understand itself.

Such is the background theory against which this play takes on special meaning for Hegel. *Antigone* is not merely the perfect tragedy; its heroine is the ideal embodiment of a principle "recognizing its opposite in its own actuality."

Hegel's reading of the play may be better philosophy than it is scholarship. There are two main points of friction between his theory and the play Sophocles wrote. First, the true representative of community in *Antigone* is not Creon but the chorus of elders, who constitute the council of state and who show some measure of sympathy for Antigone. Creon's edict is not a law of the community (though it is intended to secure the community), and his actions truly represent community values only when they arise from genuine consultation with the council of elders. Second,

Antigone is not really acknowledging her guilt at lines 925–6. I have rendered the same lines "If the gods really agree with this [Creon's judgment], / Then suffering should teach me to repent my sin." But nothing in the play suggests that the gods do agree with Creon's judgment, and nothing Antigone says implies that she believes suffering implies guilt. Her last lines, after all, are "Look what these wretched men are doing to me, / For my pure reverence!" (942–3).

Selected Bibliography

See Suggestions for Further Reading on page xxviii.

For General Readers

On Background and Interpretation

Blundell, Mary Whitlock. *Helping Friends and Harming Enemies: A Study in Sophocles and Greek Ethics.* Cambridge: Cambridge University Press, 1989.

Gilligan, Carol. *In a Different Voice: Psychological Theory and Women's Development.* Cambridge, Mass.: Harvard University Press, 1982.

Goheen, Robert. *The Imagery of Sophocles' Antigone: A Study of Poetic Language and Structure.* Princeton: Princeton University Press, 1951.

Goldhill, Simon. *Reading Greek Tragedy.* Cambridge: Cambridge University Press, 1986.

Guthrie, W. K. C. *The Sophists.* Cambridge: Cambridge University Press, 1971.

Loraux, Nicole. *Tragic Ways of Killing a Woman.* Trans. by Anthony Forster. Cambridge, Mass.: Harvard University Press, 1987.

Nussbaum, Martha. "Sophocles' *Antigone*: Conflict, Vision, and Simplification." In her *The Fragility of Goodness: Luck and Ethics in Greek Tragedy and Philosophy.* Cambridge: Cambridge University Press, 1986, pp. 51–82.

Reinhardt, Karl. *Sophocles.* 3rd ed., 1947. Trans. by Hazel Harvey and David Harvey. With an introduction by Hugh Lloyd-Jones. Oxford: Blackwell, 1979.

Seaford, Richard. *Reciprocity and Ritual: Homer and Tragedy in the Developing City-State.* Oxford: Oxford University Press, 1994.

Segal, Charles. *Tragedy and Civilization: An Interpretation of Sophocles.* Cambridge, Mass.: Harvard University Press, 1981.

———. *Sophocles' Tragic World: Divinity, Nature, Society.* Cambridge, Mass.: Harvard University Press, 1995.

Steiner, George. *Antigones: How the Antigone Legend Has Endured in Western Literature, Art, and Thought.* Oxford: Oxford University Press, 1984.

Winnington-Ingram, R. P. *Sophocles: An Interpretation.* Cambridge: Cambridge University Press, 1980.

Other Translations of *Antigone*

Blundell, Mary Whitlock. *Sophocles' Antigone*. With introduction, translation, and essay. Newburyport, Mass.: Focus Publishing, 1998.

Fagles, Robert. *The Three Theban Plays*. Introduced by Bernard Knox. New York: Viking Press, 1982.

Grene, David. *Sophocles I (Oedipus the King, Oedipus at Colonus, Antigone)*. 2nd ed. Chicago: University of Chicago Press, 1991.

Lloyd-Jones, Hugh. *Sophocles: Antigone, The Women of Trachis, Philoctetes, Oedipus at Colonus*. Cambridge, Mass.: Harvard University Press, 1994.

About Ancient Theatre

Carpenter, Thomas H., and Christopher Faraone, eds. *Masks of Dionysus*. Ithaca: Cornell University Press, 1993.

Easterling, P. E., ed. *The Cambridge Companion to Greek Tragedy*. Cambridge: Cambridge University Press, 1997.

Pickard-Cambridge, A. W. *The Dramatic Festivals of Athens*. 3rd ed. Oxford: Oxford University Press, 1990.

Winkler, John J., and Froma I. Zeitlin, eds. *Nothing to Do with Dionysus? Athenian Drama in Its Social Context*. Princeton: Princeton University Press, 1990.

For Scholars

Editions and Commentaries

Brown, Andrew. *Sophocles: Antigone*. With translation and notes. Warminster: Aris & Phillips, 1987.

Griffith, Mark. *Sophocles: Antigone*. Cambridge: Cambridge University Press, 1999.

Jebb, Sir Richard. *Sophocles: The Plays and Fragments. Part III, The Antigone. With Critical Notes, Commentary, and Translation in English Prose*. 3rd ed., 1900. Reprinted, Amsterdam: Servio, 1962.

Kamerbeek, J. C. *The Plays of Sophocles; Commentaries III: The Antigone*. Leiden: Brill, 1967.

LLoyd-Jones, H., and N. G. Wilson, *Sophoclis Fabulae*. (Text only) Oxford: Oxford University Press, 1990a.

———, and ———. *Sophoclea: Studies on the Text of Sophocles*. Oxford: Oxford University Press, 1990b.

68   SELECTED BIBLIOGRAPHY

Important Recent Studies

Bennett, Larry J., and William Blake Tyrrell. "Sophocles' *Antigone* and Funeral Oratory." *American Journal of Philology* 111 (1990): 441–56.

———, and ———. *Recapturing Sophocles' Antigone*. Lanham, Md.: Rowman and Littlefield, 1998.

Cropp, Martin. "Antigone's Final Speech (Sophocles, *Antigone* 891–928)." *Greece and Rome* 44 (1997): 137–60.

Else, Gerald F. *The Madness of Antigone*. Heidelberg: Carl Winter, 1976.

Foley, Helene P. "Tragedy and Democratic Ideology: The Case of Sophocles' *Antigone*." In Goff, Barbara, ed., *History Tragedy, Theory: Dialogues on Athenian Drama*. Austin: University of Texas Press, 1995.

———. "Antigone as Moral Agent." In Silk, M. S., ed., *Tragedy and the Tragic*. Oxford: Oxford University Press, 1996, pp. 49–73.

———. *Female Acts in Greek Tragedy*. Princeton: Princeton University Press, 2001.

Griffith, Mark. "Antigone and Her Sister(s): Embodying Women's Speech in Classical Athens." In Lardinois, André, and Laura McClure, eds., *Making Silence Speak*. Princeton: Princeton University Press, 2001, pp. 117–36.

Lewis, R. G. "An Alternative Date for Sophocles' *Antigone*." *Greek, Roman, and Byzantine Studies* 29 (1998): 35–50.

Murnaghan, Sheila. "*Antigone* 904–920 and the Institution of Marriage." *American Journal of Philology* 107 (1986): 192–207.

Neuburg, Matt. "How Like a Woman: Antigone's 'Inconsistency.'" *Classical Quarterly* 40 (1990): 54–76.

Ormand, Kirk. *Exchange and the Maiden: Marriage in Sophoclean Tragedy*. Austin: University of Texas Press, 1999.

Ostwald, Martin. "Was There a Concept of ἄγραφος νόμος in Classical Greece?" [Unwritten Law] in Lee, E. N., *et al.*, eds., *Exegesis and Argument*. Assen: Van Gorcum, 1973, pp. 70–104.

Oudemans, Theodorus C. W., and A. P. M. H. Landinois. *Tragic Ambiguity: Anthropology, Philosophy, and Sophocles' Antigone*. Leiden: 1987.

Seaford, Richard. "Tragic Money." *Journal of Hellenic Studies* 118 (1998): 119–39.

Segal, Charles Paul. "Sophocles' Praise of Man and the Conflicts of the *Antigone*." *Arion* 3 (1964): 46–66.

Sourvinou-Inwood, Christiane. "Assumptions and the Creation of Meaning: Reading Sophocles' *Antigone*." *Journal of Hellenic Studies* 109 (1989): 134–48.

Trapp, Michael. "Tragedy and the Fragility of Moral Reasoning: Response to Foley." In Silk, M. S., ed., *Tragedy and the Tragic*. Oxford: Oxford University Press, 1996, pp. 74–84.

Zeitlin, Froma. "Thebes: Theater of Self and Society in Athenian Drama." In Winkler and Zeitlin (1990), pp. 130–67.

Hegel on *Antigone*

Bradley, A. C. "Hegel's Theory of Tragedy." *Oxford Lectures on Poetry* (London 1950). Reprinted in Paolucci (1962), pp. 367–88.

Harris, H. S. *Hegel's Ladder II: The Odyssey of Spirit*. Indianapolis: Hackett Publishing Company, 1997.

Miller, A. V. , trans. *Hegel's Phenomenology of Spirit*. Oxford: Oxford University Press, 1977.

Paolucci, Anne and Henry, eds. *Hegel on Tragedy*. New York: Anchor Books: 1962.

Shannon, Daniel E., ed. *G. W. F. Hegel: Spirit; Chapter Six of Hegel's Phenomenology of Spirit*. Indianapolis: Hackett Publishing Company, 2001.

Westphal, Kenneth R. *Hegel's Epistemological Realism: A Study of the Aim and Method of Hegel's* Phenomenology of Spirit. Dordrecht: Kluwer Academic Publishers, 1989, pp. 177–78.

Wood, Allen W., ed. *Hegel: Elements of the Philosophy of Right*. Cambridge: Cambridge University Press, 1991.